DANCING ON THE RAZOR'S EDGE

A Story of Leadership
And
Triumph

Introducing a Highly Successful Leadership Concept
<u>Practicing LAP</u>

By
Arthur R. Nicholson

ISBN: 978-1-60208-190-1

First Edition 2009.

Library of Congress Card Catalog Number 2009930185

Published by SIE Global Publishing LLC 11702 Lauer Ct.,
Clinton, Maryland 20735

Sieglobalpublishing.com

Note: If you would like to have Col Nicholson speak to
your organization, write SIE Global Publishing LLC, 11702
Lauer Ct., Clinton, Maryland 20735 or Email:
nick@sieglobalpublishing.com

Printed in the USA by

FBC Publications & Printing
Ft. Pierce, FL 34982
FBCP   www.fbcpublications.com

Table of Contents

PART III Staying the Course

Dedication

I dedicate this book to my father, Charles E. Nicholson, mother, Elizabeth A. Nicholson, grandfather, Leander Nicholson and grandmother, Perlie Nicholson, all of whom helped to shape the person that I have come to be. I would also like to dedicate this work to my son Bryan. For if, those before him helped to shape me as the person I am, Bryan's existence in my life has been collectively an anchor providing stability, a mirror providing reflection, and a lighthouse providing the way forward.

My father, now deceased since 1994, helped me to not be afraid of hard work and sacrifice for others, for he surely worked hard for his family. My hands will never show the endless toil of manual labor as his, but I trust that my heart, soul, and works have captured the essence of his toil; and that you will see him through me, as you read the pages of this book.

My mother, bless her heart, was the backbone of the family: strong in character, steadfast in faith, rebellious in nature for what was right (especially where her children were concerned), and a true leader in her own right. She taught me respect for self first, and pushed me to challenge life's realities at an early age. Because she planted the seed of excellence and possibility in my mind, I am the man that I have come to be.

Leander Nicholson was a man of little formal education, but possessed a drive and passion for business that gained him respect far beyond his peers. His capacity for physical labor seemed unmatched, yet he was also blessed with a keen sense for business matters that allowed him to build a legacy in the community at large. I idolized him as a child, and even now, as a grown man when I look back, I marvel at his

5

efforts. If I accomplish in comparison to what he accomplished in his lifetime, given his circumstances, I will consider myself worthy of a nod from him in heaven. He continues to be my idol.

Mrs. Perlie Nicholson, whom I called "Big Mama," knew and loved me as Rene or Nuck, and seldom recognized my formal name Arthur. I learned giving from Big Mama, as she bore 11 children, who in turn produced more grandchildren and great grandchildren than I can count. She made me smile every time I was in her presence because of her ability to give to so many and keep a little bite of wit and humor for herself. I am smiling now just thinking of her.

These individuals deserve this dedication, for they always saw me not as I was, but as I was to be. They encouraged and supported me beyond my mistakes and shortfalls to get up and try again. Whatever I presented myself to be, they encouraged that it could be. I am, because each of them put their individual ingredients of life's successes into me to make me a whole person capable of experiencing my fullest potential. Thanks to each of you.

Being a parent in my opinion is the purest form of leadership that exists. Leadership in this form is for all the right reasons. It is not because of rank or status that the pure heart of a child follows. It is the solid foundation of trust built through the giving of love, guidance, just discipline, understanding, honesty, and the effort to be an example for one to follow. A parent's efforts to be an example does not have to be perfect, and neither have mine, but they must be above all genuine. To Bryan I say, as we always say to each other before we hang up the phone, "I think I can, so I can, and the Tiger never gives up."

Acknowledgements

To all who I do not mention below, thank you for your leadership and followership that have contributed to who I have come to be. Each one of you, by some measure, molded my thoughts and thereby my actions. This book is my acknowledgment, to each of you, for your part in making the writing of this book possible.

My sincere gratitude to:

My Son, Bryan, for your steadfast faith that I could do this.

My daughter, Tecora, for believing in me and listening to all of my crazy stories.

Mrs. Barbara Westgate, for putting me on the right track with my writing skills and your encouragement to finish this project.

Brigadier General David Goldfein, for reviewing my work and providing very candid feedback when I most needed it.

Brigadier General Harris, for the opportunity to command, and the confidence, guidance, and support that you always gave.

Colonel Roger Wujek, MD, retired, for the opportunity to grow as a young officer, and your guidance and mentorship through that growth process.

Colonel Ivan Craft, the ultimate mentor and supporter of so many. Without your sponsorship, this experience would not have come to pass. Thanks.

Colonel George Cohen, the rock, who became my confidant and guided me through the rough waters of being a commander.

Colonel Lisa Naftzger-kang (NK), a great friend and outstanding officer, for your listening ear over many years, and your confidence and support of my efforts.

Colonel Teri Muller, for your very sincere conversations on leadership and your support and review of my work.

Major Mario Cora, a superior officer who guided my thoughts and encouraged the writing of this book.

Major Thomas Connelly, my right hand man who kept it all together at the 459th AMDS.

Major Linda Dugan, a friend and officer who provided much direction, support, and encouragement in the writing of this book.

Lieutenant Edward Thomas, for your commitment and dedication to the vision of an outstanding accomplishment.

Chief Master Sergeant Regina Bulkhalter, for putting me on the right track and mentoring me through the leadership maze.

Senior Master Sergeant Janet Faust, for the staying power that you so demonstrated and for your support while I learned the art of command.

Master Sergeant Taft Mitchell, for your very candid review and feedback on my work.

Technical Sergeant Bullock-Labaran, for your keen insight of people and situations which kept me grounded as a new commander.

A1C Clement Addo for your ideas, support, and review of my work.

Members of the 459th AMDS, for enduring me as we formed, stormed, and finally got it together to perform at an outstanding level.

Mr. Stephen Hicks, my supervisor and friend, for the many stories we shared on leadership and your review/feedback of my work.

Mr. Severen O'Bryan, one of my first mentors in the Air Force, and a very dear friend, for your inspiration and confidence in me for so many years.

Mr. Kerwin Lay, for your mentorship and friendship which continues to encourage me.

Ms. Linda Holton, for your expert guidance through all the phases of writing this book.

Ms. Karen Kuhnline, a friend and colleague for listening to the stories and providing feedback.

Ms. Sherry Curtis, for your friendship and providing sincere feedback and insight to my writing.

Foreword to

"Dancing on the Razor's Edge"

By Colonel Roger A. Wujek (Retired)

For civilian readers, an Air Force Medical Squadron that fails its Health Services Inspection (HSI) is a rare and significant event. It is looked upon as a failure of leadership. It places the Air Wing in jeopardy of successful mission deployment, and an unsatisfactory score usually portents a death knoll for the career of its commander.

If you were a recently promoted Colonel anticipating your first command, this position would not be the place to start your command career, unless you were a person of exceptional commitment, energy, and resilience, and a career student of leadership. Such was the case for Colonel Arthur Nicholson, a Medical Services Corps Officer (MSC) who served in a variety of responsible positions over his 32-year career, but never as a commander of an Air Force Reserve Squadron, and certainly not of a medical squadron which recently failed their HSI. It would take exceptional leadership and unwavering commitment just to get a "*Satisfactory*" on the next HSI. Perhaps with superb leadership from an experienced commander it would be possible to eke out an "*Excellent.*" But for a new commander, in his first command position, with only 18 months of preparation, to rate an "*Outstanding*" is, well…

LEGENDARY.

In this book "Dancing on the Razor's Edge," Colonel Nicholson shares his leadership technique, LAP that was so successful in not simply mobilizing a demoralized squadron to do well, but rather *inspiring* them to a world-class, over-the-top performance that no one expected.

A "satisfactory" might have been good enough, but **good** is the enemy of **best,** and this squadron of exceptional people led by an exceptional leader is a case study validating the effectiveness of practicing Leadership, Accountability, and Professionalism—LAP. It's a solid program to follow for dependable results in any organization of any size.

Preface

This book is a powerful success story about leadership, the practice of leadership, accountability, and professionalism, (LAP), and the extraordinary turnaround of a failing organization. The organization could have been any organization, but it was an actual Air Force medical examination unit that overcame both failure and probable elimination. The unit excelled to outstanding success given the injection and practice of some fundamental leadership techniques that galvanized the unit personnel. The principles and concepts of leadership, accountability, and professionalism were packaged into a phrase called "Practicing (LAP)." This phrase became the measuring stick for personnel to gauge each other's leadership/followership behavior, and commitment to our stated vision. Along with practicing LAP, we applied discipline and old-fashioned hard work to get the mission accomplished.

The topic of leadership has been studied and written about for many years and on many levels. I have embraced much of the work and writings on leadership and have successfully utilized these principles throughout my career. Although practicing these principles of leadership yielded the desired results, there was always something missing that addressed the lasting effects of leadership. As I continued to grow through my leader/follower experiences in my career, I developed an approach "practicing LAP" that both yields desired results and sustains those results beyond mission success. This book is therefore about the packaging of some very basic techniques and disciplines of leading that facilitated the extraordinary success of an organization.

Accordingly, this book is neither an autobiography nor an instructional manual for practicing leadership. However, it is a very intriguing story about a particular unit, in its darkest moments, and a commander growing together to achieve great success. At times, throughout the book, I have shared very personal and sensitive situations in an effort to expose the origins of my leadership development, its practice, and the impact that it has had on my tenure as a Commander.

I am writing about this phenomenal experience because I feel compelled to share the leadership lessons learned with potential or seasoned leaders, both military, and civilian. My hope is that we may see ourselves in a place mentally (virtually), before we get there in reality. Additionally, I trust it will help each of us hit the replay button to re-familiarize ourselves with our own lessons learned.

During the planning and writing of this book, I went through the process of laying out the lessons learned, and subsequently organized them in the form of chapters. The chapters are laid out to reflect, sequentially, the significant events that took place over an eighteen-month period. From a leadership perspective, eighteen months may seem like a very short time for some people, but to others who have been in the trenches of a highly intense, do or die, win or lose it all situation, eighteen months can feel like a lifetime.

Chapter 1 discusses the decision of accepting/taking Command (the realization). No matter the circumstances surrounding your particular situation, accepting command (military or civilian) is one of those significant emotional events that you never forget.

Chapter 2 explores establishing the vision (your vision) with the organization, which is something we all should do as soon as possible after taking command, if not before. It is critical for those we are leading to know up front where we are leading them and what the end game/state is going to look like when we get there.

Chapter 3 addresses gaining the trust (the permission to lead). No one goes into a leadership position with a green light to lead from everyone. For most leaders, it is at best a yellow light of caution until we have gained our follower's trust by some measure. A leader must be able to produce early results, and be able to deal with distrust.

Chapter 4 supports the premise that becoming a great leader is part of becoming a great follower through the development of Followership. Followership is the benefactor of a leader's conscious focus on mentoring and growing their replacements. I will also discuss, specifically, challenges of developing followership in the 459th Aerospace Medicine Squadron (AMDS).

Chapter 5 explores making the tough calls (thick face, black heart) which involves a mindset for executing in a timely, eliberate, and professional manner. The thick face, black heart approach is offered as a method for living and leading on a positive proactive level.

Chapter 6 deals with "The Mission (from broken to bench mark)." Simply put, we were not accomplishing the mission and finding a way to make it work was the only option. The challenges of understanding the mission, and then leading the way to building a benchmark organization are discussed in this chapter.

Chapter 7 discusses The Committed Few vs. The Uncommitted Many concepts as they pertain to leading and leadership. The leader must address both groups in a way that keeps the committed few focused on the vision, and the uncommitted few believing in the vision enough to be a part of the team that affects the vision. The leader must inspire both groups.

Chapter 8 deals with Being a Part of Something Great, which is the effort of individuals committing to a perceived outcome, based on an inspired vision. An individual's existence in an organization takes on new or renewed meaning when they are sincerely engaged in a cause that they believe is greater than self.

Chapter 9 develops the concept of Practicing LAP as a package and as an action. The package (leadership, accountability, professionalism) facilitates a leadership culture that is servant based, relational, visionary, and inspiring. Practicing LAP the action, is a way of living and leading as an individual.

Chapter 10 Leadership the first tenet of LAP is explored in terms of what is means to practice leadership under the umbrella of LAP. Leadership is important and necessary in these changing and challenging times. Understanding how to practice leadership as a component of LAP is critical to a leader maximizing the practice of LAP.

Chapter 11 Accountability as a component of practicing LAP is a grounding mechanism that supports a leader's expressions of leadership and professionalism. The impact of developing accountability on individual and organizational levels is examined.

Chapter 12 Professionalism, the last tenet of "Practicing LAP", is defined and developed in this chapter. Professionalism is the tip of the iceberg of "Practicing LAP". The lasting affects of practicing professionalism are addressed with regard effectiveness and influence.

Chapter 13 is about turning the corner from failure to success and being forever patient. My experience has taught me that patience is a fundamental virtue needed for effective leadership. Turning the corner from failure to success can be a very frustrating experience, but when it happens, it is a significant emotional event.

Chapter 14 is the subject of holding it all together (keeping eyes on the target). It is like the seventh inning stretch of the baseball game. The teams literally catch their breath, make the necessary adjustments to hold on to the lead, or take the lead to win the game.

In Chapter 15 "the Vision Becomes a Reality," (the rolling O) describes the moment of success. It describes the feeling at that exact moment of realizing the success of one's goals. It also describes what it means to be a part of something great.

Chapter 16 "Next" (adjusting the vision), addresses the subject of not resting or lying back on your accomplishments. The mission is ever changing and a leader's obligation is to adjust the vision to ensure continued successful mission accomplishment.

The material in this book is written for individuals at a number of levels along the path of leadership, as this book is targeted to all who aspire to be leaders. We must recognize that we should never stop striving to learn about leadership. It is a continuing and evolving process. Through the ideas and experiences highlighted in this book, it is my goal that this story will give you another perspective from which to appreciate the practice of leadership in any area of your daily lives.

As you read the pages of this book, my desire is that it will inspire potential leaders to step up to the awesome responsibility of leading. To those already in leadership positions, may it reinvigorate your excitement to lead, teach and mentor.

My prayer here is that you will experience this book as I intended it to be, a preparatory tool, a stimulus to lead, and a framework for reflecting on your own leadership experiences, through the sharing of my own experiences of command.

Practicing leadership, accountability, and professionalism (LAP) is a neatly packaged concept that can work in any organization and for any mission. As leaders, we must all strive to find and realize the leader within, for we simply do not know the exact moment that we will be thrust into a leadership role. Until then, seek, learn, and meditate on your leadership, accountability, and professionalism skills as you embark on your journey of realizing the leader within.

Introduction

Imagine taking over an organization that you knew was in trouble only to receive a call from your mentor apologizing for directing and encouraging you to take the position, because it turns out that the situation is much worse (a bigger opportunity) than expected. It happened to me and it could happen to you. This was the start of the **Dance On The Razor's EDGE**.

If you are an aspiring leader, willing to accept increasing challenges, you too will find yourself faced with what seems to be an overwhelming and/or impossible situation. However, do not despair, you can lead beyond what seems to be a no win situation. How do I know that you can? I know you can because I am no different from you! With the leadership techniques and concepts described in this book, along with a dedicated group of individuals, an organization was led beyond its darkest moments.

I have concluded that "leadership, accountability, and professionalism" are fundamental concepts, which if practiced, shape one's behavior on their way to successful leadership positions in all areas of life. I say this because in the situation that I have described above, there were only two key, senior personnel changes, the Commander and the Chief Nurse. With only those two changes, a revived and inspired group of individuals incorporated the practice of LAP and transformed an organization. This experience speaks to the fact that leaders truly influence/inspire, however, it is dedicated, inspired people that make it happen. In the restaurant business, we have all heard that it is about location, location, location. In a situation like the one described above, notwithstanding the undeniable people factor, it is about leadership, leadership, leadership!

A colleague recently asked me, "what is leadership?" to which I replied, "Leadership is the essence of influencing and inspiring others." He followed with the question, "Then what is leadership for you?" I replied, "Leadership is about leaving others in a better place." I further explained that beyond executing the organizational mission, leadership is helping others realize and develop their fullest potential as leaders in whatever profession they may find themselves.

William A. Cohen, Ph.D., Major General, USAFR, Retired, wrote in his book "The New Art of the Leader," "to help others perform ethically and to the maximum level that they are able to accomplish any mission, project, or task is the highest expression of good leadership."[1]

I must say that after reading Dr. Cohen's book, and knowing of his vast experience in the field of leadership, I was quite pleased that our thoughts on this aspect of leadership were very similar and converged on the same points.

To help others find the leader within, realize, and develop their fullest potential as a leader, are the reasons I decided to share my story with you. This account of my tour as a Commander, reveals how others found their leadership stride as well, which helped turn around an organization that was literally on the brink of extinction.

As you experience this extraodinary story of success, my wish is that you will project yourself into its leadership situations or reflect on your own experiences to learn and gain a different perspective of how to best recognize, develop, and enhance the leader within.

We all have the leader within, that if recognized, developed, and practiced to its fullest potential, will propel our existence to the maximum of whatever endeavor we propose. No matter what your profession, in the story that follows, I trust you will find and realize the leader within; and that it inspires you to build something great through the concept of "Practicing LAP," Leadership, Accountability, and Professionalism.

"A journey of a thousand miles begins with a single step."
Lao-tzu, The Way of Lao-tzu
          Chinese philosopher (604 BC - 531 BC)

Chapter 1

Taking Command

At the beginning of any endeavor, it is smart to start with the end in mind. That is just what I did when I took over as the Commander of the 459th Aerospace Medicine Squadron at Andrews Air Force Base, Maryland, in January 2007. After twenty-four months serving as Commander, and with the end of that tour in the rear view mirror, I can now tell a story of monumental proportions that will forever positively influence the lives of those who lived it.

459th Aerospace Medicine Squadron

The 459th Aerospace Medicine Squadron (AMDS) is an Air Force Reserve medical squadron comprised of over 80 personnel, with the mission of ensuring that all Air Force members in the 459th Air Refueling Wing are medically fit to fight. "Fit to fight" meant that all Airmen in the Wing were medically ready to go to war at any time. This was a daunting responsibility because the entire Wing's medical readiness rested squarely on the 459th AMDS. The unit personnel consisted of flight doctors, nurses, medical technicians, medical administrators, and a host of other medical specialists that supported the physical examination process for more than 1,300 personnel. The unit's performance history had been marginal to satisfactory since its existence, in part due to several top leadership changes in past years. It failed its most recent Health Services Inspection in June of 2006. The Health Services Inspection administered by the Air Force Inspection Agency (AFIA), is a critical inspection that assesses the executive management of the organization and validates its processes. When an organization fails a Health Services Inspection, a re-inspection will occur within 24 months. A failure of this type carries with it two obvious conclusions; a failure of leadership and a failure of the mission. It puts a leader's ability to command in question with peers, superiors, and ultimately himself. It is, in most cases, career limiting, if not career ending for the commander. The failure further degrades the peacetime and wartime operational capability of the unit and the wing. It limits training opportunities of a unit's members and severely cripples a unit's contribution to its wartime taskings. In particular, from a corporate point of view, this failure presented an opportunity to dissolve the 459th AMDS, a marginally operating unit, and incorporate its mission into another more stable unit. Additionally, this failure was the first failure of a medical unit in the history of the 4th Air Force, the parent organization to which the Wing answered. Needless to say, the pressure was on.

Selected for Command

To articulate the breadth and depth of being a commander, I have included an explanation from Lt. Col. Eileen Isola, Commander, 463d Operations Support Squadron. *"It is sometimes frustrating to try to explain to someone-military or civilian-what this "being a commander" thing is all about, simply because they cannot possibly understand the depth, complexity, and hours involved. Nor could you. I am a teacher, counselor, rescuer, parent, mentor, confessor, judge and jury, executioner, cheerleader, coach, nudger, butt-kicker, hugger, social worker, lawyer, shrink, doctor, analyst, budgeter, allowance giver, career planner, assignment getter, inspector, critic, scheduler, planner, shopper, social organizer, party thrower, and absolutely as*

often as possible- sacrificial lamb. I am my squadron's
commander, and will only do this job one way while I'm in it
... whatever it takes to serve them."[2]

Given the possible roles a commander can be involved in, given the mission and personnel responsibilities, the 24/7 on the job expectation, sacrifice of family, and living in a fish bowl, one can only ask why anyone would aspire to this position. Simply put, the opportunity to command is a tremendous honor and responsibility, and unquestionably one of the most significant and rewarding roles in an Air Force career. Accordingly, command is reserved for those individuals exhibiting only the highest levels of integrity, selflessness, and excellence.[3]

My opportunity to command came from Colonel Stayce Harris (now Brigadier General) then Wing Commander of the 459th Air Refueling Wing at Andrews AFB, MD. I was very apprehensive about this opportunity, as it was with a type of medical unit that I had no direct experience. Adding to my apprehension was that I was interviewing with a true legend in Brigadier General Harris. She was celebrated as the first African American female to command a Wing, and she was an accomplished Air Force pilot and Captain with a major Airline. I had only met her once at a conference, by introducing myself, not knowing that one day I would be sitting in front of her interviewing for a Commander position in her Wing. Brigadier General Harris is one of those rare individuals that inspire you to give of yourself and perform on levels that you never thought were achievable.

The interview went exceptionally well given that Colonel Harris was looking for a set of criteria in a Commander that represented leadership, integrity, initiative, and command presence; which I was able to convey. In return, she pledged support and provided the top cover that a new commander truly needs to be successful in turning a unit around. There is something about being in the presence of someone that you truly admire. I am sure that you have felt this at one time or another; it is the desire to succeed that comes from the energy and the admiration of a person and leader such as Brigadier General Stayce D. Harris. Shortly after the interview, Brigadier General Harris offered me the position as the commander of the 459th Aerospace Medicine Squadron, and I quickly accepted.

The Realization

In taking command, the desire, the opportunity, and the decision finally put me squarely in the driver's seat. This is the moment of stark realization that the failure or success of the organization depends on the failure or success of your leadership. This moment is very familiar to leaders who accept leadership roles in various organizations, civilian or military. It is the decisive moment of truth. Can I really do it? Do I have what it takes? Will they follow my lead? What have I done? Although I had survived very dangerous life threatening deployments to Kuwait, Saudi Arabia (Operation Desert Storm), and Kirkuk Iraq (Operation Iraqi Freedom), these are all questions that invariably ran through my mind. These and other thoughts were part of my realization as I took command of the 459th Aerospace Medicine Squadron (AMDS) at Andrews AFB, Maryland, 3 January, 2007.

To say that taking command was a rude awakening would be an over kill, but it was a "true" awakening. Those who have taken over organizations know exactly what I am saying. Up to this point in my career, I had trained for an operational mission where I took my skills to the fight, wherever that was, and took care of those fighting. Now my charge was to ensure that airmen were medically fit to fight, which was at the other end of the spectrum of my 30 plus years of training; a totally different paradigm.

I have started and operated several small businesses from tax preparation to a restaurant, and knew the pressures of running a business; but this task before me was somehow different from any other endeavor that I had undertaken. Let me explain; this was to be my first command in the military and I had inherited a squadron that had been assessed by inspection-NOT READY! The failure of an organizational inspection affects the organization internally and externally on all levels. I will not dwell on the multitude of considerations that had to be addressed, but it is safe to say that a seasoned leader would have his or her hands full with this situation, and I was not a seasoned leader as a Commander. Get the picture? I knew that I was diving into an abyss taking over this unit, but to me it represented an opportunity, and the only way out, was up. Even though this situation was one that I would not have wished on anyone, the challenge was indeed an opportunity to command, and I wanted very much to test my skills at that level.

To prepare for this daunting endeavor, I did as I usually do when faced with a similar situation; I researched it. Since the age of thirteen, I have read motivational and leadership books, and at this point, I needed to remember all that I had read. Fortunately, before leaving 4th Air Force, a very dear friend and seasoned Chief Master Sergeant (CMSgt) Regina Bulkhalter presented me with a book entitled "Rules & Tools for Leaders, A Down-to-Earth Guide to Effective Managing," authored by Major General Perry M. Smith, PhD, USAF (Retired).[4] Timing is everything, and I received that book at precisely the right time. I encourage anyone taking over an organization to read this book as well as other books that help to prepare one to lead an organization.

Drawing on Lessons Learned

In unfamiliar territory as I was, I relied on lessons learned as a civil pilot since 1983. I had come to appreciate the fact that if I did not know exactly what I was doing when I got into a different airplane, following a checklist was a great approach, (the only approach), and that is what the book Rules & Tools for Leaders provided on the front end of this endeavor. When my mentor presented the opportunity to me, one of the first questions that I asked was if the members were competent and willing? When he assured me that they were both, I thought to myself, all that was missing was leadership. In hindsight, that was probably a hefty (inexperienced) assumption on my part, especially having never met anyone in the organization and never having a command. One thing that I did know from prior experiences was that the organization was most likely demoralized from the failure, unsure about the future, and apprehensive about a new commander and his intentions. To mitigate those concerns to some extent, one of the first things that I expressed to the unit members after taking command was that we, not I, would jointly figure out the way forward. I also established my credibility beyond the confidence implied by Brigadier General Harris' choice by sharing my history of military experience of over 30 years. Additionally I asked for time to gain their trust as their commander, which I will discuss in detail in chapter 3.

Establishing Presence

"Presence" means one's ability to project a sense of ease, poise, or self-assurance.[5] I made an effort to project a sense of ease, poise, or self-assurance and more when I met with the outgoing commander during his last days. That was a very intense and emotional week as he transitioned out of the very coveted position that I was to assume. As we arranged our schedules to facilitate a transfer of corporate knowledge, neither of us really knew what to expect from each other, or what reactions would unfold during this very awkward time. **(Another opportunity to Dance On The Razor's EDGE.)** Our first meeting was very cordial, yet there was a sense of distance between us with regard to information exchange. As the week progressed, a very interesting thing occurred in this transition of power. A healthy respect for the position of commander consumed us both. Any guards that we had individually built up fell away as we both focused on what it was going to take to make the unit viable again. The need to present a show of presence gave way to a natural presence between us. Through the natural presence that evolved, I began to understand what being a commander is not about. It is not about money, status, position, or any shallow attributes that can be attached to a position of that nature. It is about the honor and privilege of serving, leading, inspiring people to accomplish the mission, and simultaneously transforming individuals into all that they can be. The bottom line was that by the end of that week, the outgoing commander was convinced that I, the incoming commander, was first sincere about taking care of his people, and secondly very focused about accomplishing the mission.

There were a multitude of actions that I accomplished during my first appearance with the members of the organization. All were geared to establishing a genuine sense of presence. As a believer that first impressions are lasting, I initially established a presence that reflected the gravity of the situation at hand, and projected a sense of confidence that united, we could get this airplane flying again. All of the aforementioned was my stark realization that I had made a decision that ultimately placed me in a position to affect the mission of an organization, and maybe more importantly, individually affect the members of that organization. I then had a real sense that what I did next could have a profound impact on the success or failure of both. Remember, it is all about leadership, leadership, leadership!

Chapter 1 Leadership Takeaways

- Take time to decide if you truly desire to be in a leadership position. Do you have what it takes?

- Always be prepared for the opportunity.

- Accept the challenge wholeheartedly.

- Research, study, and familiarize yourself with the organization that you are about to command.

- Begin with the end in mind.

- Draw on past experiences and lessons learned, good and bad.

- Establish presence.

- It is all about leadership, leadership, leadership.

****

**"Leadership is going where
there is no direction
And leaving a path for
others to follow."
~ARN~**

****

"Most people grow up and conform within the parameters that have been set before them, then, there are those who make their own parameters; these are the Dreamers"

Arthur R. Nicholson

Chapter 2

Establishing the Vision

My Vision

My vision for this organization was simple yet daunting; it was for the unit to be performing at an outstanding level by the time we were due for the follow-up Health Service's Inspection. When I took command on 3 January, 2007, the unit was scheduled to be re-inspected in 18 months. The accomplishment of an outstanding rating would indeed be a part of something great. It would have the status of greatness because a unit is expected to score at least satisfactory, and to come from a failure to a grade of excellent is beyond expectations. However, to achieve an outstanding score would be in the stratosphere of expectations. It would also shatter the shackles of failure and mediocrity that the unit had experienced. This vision supported the Wing and Unit's strategic vision of "Warriors medically ready; Medics warrior ready" as well.

Establishing the vision for any organization is at least a three-prong process that encompasses creating the vision in your own mind first. Your vision is the compass that everyone uses to proceed in the right direction for the organization. Having the vision crystal clear and firmly imbedded in your mind, heart, and spirit before you assume command is crucial to the direction you will take the organization. Imparting or communicating your vision is the next step, and is akin to fueling the hearts and minds of those you need to accomplish the vision. Adding more fuel of the highest octane available translates to communicating the vision with breath and depth to the organization, which will determine how fast you will realize it, and how long the vision will be sustained. Finally, continuously cultivating your vision across and into every level of the organization until it becomes crystal clear in the minds of those you are leading is paramount to achieving the goal. Cultivating here means working the vision, putting it into action, and walking the talk as a leader. Once this point is reached, staying on course is like that of placing an aircraft on autopilot where periodic checks are all that is necessary to keep the aircraft on track.

A leader who creates, communicates, and cultivates his or her vision with passion, sincerity and inclusiveness will raise the consciousness of those they lead, and ultimately lead the organization to greatness. This process is the essence of inspiring those you lead to greatness.

Anchoring Support for The Vision

To anchor support for the vision, one of the first things that I did after taking command was to interview everyone that was in a position of leadership. If a person was in charge of a program or in charge of people, a one-on-one meeting was scheduled with them to established a rapport, understand who they were, what program they were in charge of, and lay out my expectations of them. These interviews served to facilitate and solidify support for the vision as a by-product of my understanding the needs and aspirations of those who I was to lead. I expressed to each interviewee that I would create an environment that would spurn an opportunity for them to succeed. In essence, I was saying that I would empower them to lead. As leaders of organizations, we must understand that our visions will take the efforts of others to make them happen. Consequently, the sooner everyone is on one accord supporting the vision, the sooner the vision will be realized.

One of the individuals that I promptly decided to speak with was Colonel George Cohen, who was the unit's top-flight surgeon and chief of Aerospace medicine. In his civilian capacity, Dr. Cohen is also an accomplished Dermatologist. As a well-seasoned physician and reservist, Colonel Cohen represented much more than his job title indicated, given his significant number of years serving this Unit. A flight surgeon is the only person who can make the determination to take a person off flight status or determine that an airman is medically unfit for duty. Accordingly, airmen are, at the very least, apprehensive about seeing a flight surgeon for any reason. Dr. Cohen knew the mission, loved to fly, and was not afraid to call it as he saw it. Although flyers usually avoided seeing flight surgeons at all cost, when Dr. Cohen said "no go," flyers and others respected his judgment, because they knew he had assessed to the maximum degree the medical impact on the operational mission. I too gained a high degree of confidence in Colonel Cohen during our first interview. He was a straight shooter who did not mix his words, and knew the unit and the wing missions inside out. Dr. Cohen had also gained a level of trust inside and outside the organization which meant that he was the anchor. He quickly became a confidante with whom I verified and validated most of my decisions and direction. Identifying such an individual in your organization is crucial to your success as a leader.

Sharing the Vision

The goal of sharing the vision with others is that they will embrace it as their own and become as passionate as you are about it. The first opportunity that I had to share the vision with the entire organization was on Saturday, 2 February, 2007 during the regular Unit Training Assembly (UTA), and I sensed that this would be a pivotal event. Some will understand what I am about to say and others will come to understand it. There are instances in life when if you are truly in touch with the leader within; you will be conscious of those pivotal moments as they present themselves. The key to capturing all that there is in that moment hinges on the ability to project the moment before it arrives. That ability is called intuition, vision, prophecy, cognitive thinking, or just simply listening to your inner voice. The following are the ideals and concepts that I shared with them to create the vision in their minds, and inspire the vision in their hearts.

The Committed Few

The "committed few" is a concept that captures and labels the commitment and effort of those who are always willing to give their best. My goal for sharing this concept was to capture the hearts and minds of those who were ready to embrace the change of leadership and a new vision. Thomas J. Watson, Jr., once said: "...the basic philosophy, spirit, and drive of an organization have far more to do with its relative achievements than do technological or economic resources, organizational structure, innovation, and timing. All these things weigh heavily in success. But they are, I think, transcended by how strongly the people in the organization believe in its basic precepts and how faithfully they carry them out."[6] A "Committed Few" with an inspired vision, over time, can affect many. Details of this concept will be expanded on in chapter 7.

Being a Part of Something Great

Without any fanfare, I shared with the unit that we could be an outstanding organization in the next 18 months, and the accomplishment would indeed be a part of something great. Being a part of something great as I defined it, is being a part of a team with a vision, which is striving to do something great. On great teams that stand the test of time, no individual on the team is bigger than the team. Everyone contributes at his or her maximum potential and is aware that realizing the vision depends on each other working together as a team. The passion that we bring to the team, and the vision, equals commitment, and is the foundation for striving to do something great.

I also shared my experience of a former organization that received an outstanding score on its recent inspection and in fact, two of the three units in the group received an outstanding rating under the leadership of Colonel Wujek (Retired). I told them of being in the room when the score was revealed, and everyone broke out in cheers and tears, and it was a great moment. Boldly I suggested that we too could experience the same, and more if we became a team focused on a common goal. The common goal was to be a part of something great. This concept will be expanded on in chapter 8. I introduced one additional concept that was the corner stone of my overall vision.

Practicing LAP

The last concept that I shared that day was developed over many years of experience with individuals, organizations, and situations. Leadership, Accountability, and Professionalism are all subjects that I have studied, practiced, and evaluated throughout my civilian and military career. As a commander, I wanted to develop a way to capture these behaviors into one phrase or theme. One day I had an epiphany, and the phrase "Practicing LAP" was born. Practicing LAP is a concept conceived with the intent to inspire the continuous development of the leader within each of us. Mastering the practice of LAP is a manifestation of natural leadership from within, that is servant based, relational, visionary, and inspiring. Details of this concept will be expanded on in chapter 9.

The practice of leadership, accountability, and professionalism under the umbrella of "practicing LAP is expanded in chapters 10, 11, and 12 respectively.

I realized at my first full meeting with the organization, that I raised the bar high. However, this was done to see who would stand up, be counted as the committed few, and be open minded enough to explore the concepts that were presented. At that first meeting, I used stories, introduced concepts, and presented challenges to create a vision of where the unit could go in the next 18 months; achieving an outstanding rating on our next Health Service's Inspection. Soon after that meeting, the members themselves put it all together, and we became the unit known as "The Committed Few Practicing LAP - A Part of Something Great."

Chapter 2 Leadership Takeaways

- Establishing the vision for any organization is at least a three-prong process.
  - o Have a precise vision firmly in mind when you take over.
  - o Communicate your vision.
  - o Continuously cultivate your vision with breath and depth into every level of the organization.

- A leader who creates, communicates, and cultivates his or her vision with passion, sincerity and inclusiveness will raise the consciousness of those they lead and ultimately lead the organization to greatness.

- As leaders of organizations, we must understand that our visions will take the efforts of others to make them happen.

- Anchor support for your vision by getting to know your people (find your confidant within the organization).

- Create an environment for success.

- The goal of sharing your vision with others is that they will embrace it as their own and become as passionate as you are about it.

- Win the hearts and minds of those who depend on your leadership.

- Raise the bar of expectation to achieve excellence.

- A "Committed Few" with an inspired vision, over time, can affect many.

- Being a part of something great is being a part of a team with a vision, which is striving to do something great.

- Mastering the practice of LAP is a manifestation of natural leadership from within, that is servant based, relational, visionary, and inspiring.

"You are only worth the sum total of your commitment, and the worth of that commitment is based on the level at which you commit"

Arthur R. Nicholson, (Aug 1993)

Chapter 3

Gaining the Trust

This chapter is one of the most important chapters in this book. As leaders, we can possess all of the character traits that make up a great leader, but without the single element of trust, we will be failures. This is a bold statement, but it is true. "Trust indicates a depth and a sense of assurance that is based on strong but not logically-conclusive evidence, or based on the character, ability, or truth shown by someone or something over time or across situations. Trust breeds confidence and conviction."[7] If you as a leader do not pay attention to gaining the trust of those you are charged to lead, you are doomed to lose before the race has even begun. Gaining their trust is the essence of the permission to lead on an individual level as well as mutually, on an organizational level. The bottom line on how to gain the trust of those you lead, is to lead with **integrity**.

The Permission to Lead

All leaders face the challenge of gaining the permission to lead from those they are charged to lead when taking over an organization. I knew I would not have everyone's trust immediately, while there were those who trusted me right away as Brigadier General Harris's choice as Commander of the 459th AMDS. How does one handle this situation? My technique was to ask for time to prove myself worthy of their trust. Two things immediately occurred as by-products of hat gesture. First, individuals were empowered by the act of giving them a choice to accept or reject me as their leader, based on the trustworthiness that I displayed (actions).[8] This is important to the concept of servant leadership in that it places the leader in a position of proving him or herself through action. The leader is saying, let me show you who and what I am. Let me give before I receive; and let me show that I will go the extra mile before I ask anyone to take even the first step. This is the essence of servant leadership and leading with integrity. It also cultivates an environment that is receptive to change. Change takes time, and not everyone is ready for change at the same time. Accordingly, appealing for time to prove one's self creates the opportunity for the occurrence and acceptance of change.

The following example illustrates how difficult it is to gain trust, which equates to the permission to lead. This occurred between one of the full time staff and myself. This person held the senior position of the full time staff, and represented the Commander in all matters of running the organization. To establish open communication during my absence from the unit, I set up specific times during the month to talk with this individual about all aspects of the organization. During one of our conversations, I sensed a reluctance to openly communicate and share information. I stated my concern, to which came a surprising reply. She said, "I am not use to talking with the Commander on such matters, and am very uncomfortable doing so." I was very surprised to hear this, given that we had talked during our initial interview, and it seemed that we had struck a meeting of the minds. Her role, and its importance to the organization was acknowledged, and the importance of the collaborative relationship that we needed to establish to move the organization toward our stated goals was conveyed. After several hours of conversation, the root cause inhibiting the relationship that we needed between us, revealed itself; trust. Leadership, peers, and subordinates because of their lack of confidence in her ability to lead and manage the organization, had marginalized this individual, notwithstanding her position. She was not trusted, which manifested into her withdrawal of opinion and involvement in critical issues that she needed to be engaged in. Trust is a double-edged sword, and ultimately, she had built up a wall of distrust for leadership. Granted, she was not the template of the ultimate leader that we have all come to expect through teachings or experience. That is why it is justified to throw the template out the window and not simply judge the contents of a book by its cover. To know a person's character, is to know them from inside out; and we as leaders, must develop the patience to get to know our people. What she did have was a willing spirit, an untapped reservoir of ability, and a working knowledge of the organization.

With that assessment, we began to work on the one element that was necessary to build and sustain our relationship----trust. I realized that she lacked self-confidence, which had eroded over time, and she needed to be genuinely valued. We devised a plan for her professional development, and committed to being open and honest with each other about our feelings, expectations, and shortcomings. Getting to the desired state of complete trust in each other was not easy, and we suffered some setbacks along the way. However, to be trusted, and valued were critical to her development, and to our relationship. In the end, she was standing tall, more confident than before, and more trusting of leadership, peers and subordinates. We can both say that we grew through that experience, and the outcome was worth the struggle of the journey.

Creating an Environment for Success

Leaders, if you want an organizational environment that fosters success, you have to create it. You should quickly embrace this task upon taking over an organization. Although you cannot do it alone, the creation starts with the leader. An organizational climate survey is a great way to start. A climate survey is a suggested tool for gathering data about the emotional health of an organization and its personnel.[9] Usually a climate survey is recommended within the first six months of a top leadership change. Climate surveys must be performed professionally, and preferably by a trusted source. Leaders are usually surprised by the outcome, but leaders should study the data and deal with the outcomes head on.

We had to deal with some devastating trends (definite showstoppers) revealed in a unit climate survey that I authorized during my first six months of command. One thing that I learned is that leaders will not always be acutely aware of the undercurrent of activity in an organization. Even in the face of the obvious, a leader's view of the organization is sometimes like viewing a duck moving across a body of water. On the surface, everything appears smooth and graceful; while beneath the surface, just out of eyesight, the duck is paddling with great effort.

The same situation occurs in organizations, especially when leaders are focused on the mission. We are sometimes naively blind to the environment that must support the success of the mission. Another way of relating to this blind spot of leadership is to understand that there is always an undercurrent in the organizational waters that you never see. However, you will certainly experience it when you dive in.

The results of our survey revealed that we had individual and organizational trust issues, cultural disconnects, and some perceived discrimination. Some of the written comments were very specific and needed immediate attention. Although I was completely stunned by the results of the survey, I sensed the urgency of addressing each issue and stating my position on them as a Commander. We also brought in professional help to address the legal implications of offenders of any type of discrimination. When a leader finds him or herself in this situation, you have to be firm, sincere, and convincing with your message. It must be known that you are serious, and that you are in no way bluffing about what you will do if you encounter someone in violation of your stated policies. In short, walk the talk.

As with any challenge, there is opportunity, and we recognized the need and benefit of establishing internal communication building sessions, taught by our own members. These sessions were instrumental in bringing awareness to the cultural, religious, and ethical rich environment of our organization. It also gave individuals a platform to express openly, concerns that they might have with any aspect of the organization. The sessions ultimately served to create an environment of inclusiveness, and value, on both individual, and organizational levels.

Creating an environment that is conducive to the individual success of your members should also support, and be strongly linked to the success of the organization. During the initial interviews, I assured each member that I was committed to creating an environment in which they could succeed. To remain true to my commitment, I had to get to know the strengths and challenges of as many people in the organization as possible. Getting to know your people is the only way that we as leaders can genuinely make the effort to place them in challenging situations and positions that set them up for success. When I say set them up for success, I mean growth situations as leaders and mentors where the outcome will benefit the individual, as well as the organization and the mission. Again, to be successful in this endeavor, you must make every effort to know your people.

Organizational Trust

Fostering, and recognizing an environment of trust internally and externally to your organization is just as critical to organizational success as building trust into one-on-one relationships. In our case, internal and external organizational trust issues existed which were inhibitors to the successful accomplishment of our goals. Organizational trust can be defined as the integrated judgment of one group that another group will be honest, meet commitments, and will not take advantage of others (Bradach & Eccles, 1989; Cummings & Bromily, 1996).[10] Others view organizational trust as an exchange between individuals within the construct of an organizational context (Barney &Hansen, 1994; Butler, 1991; Zaheer et al., 1998).[11] In the book "The Trusted Leader" Robert Galford and Anne Seibold describe three specific categories of trust within an organization:[12]

- Strategic trust – trust in the organization's mission, strategy, and ability to succeed.
- Organizational trust – trust that the organization's policies will be fairly administered and implemented as stated.
- Personal trust – trust that subordinates place in their manager to be fair and to look out for their interests.

Accordingly, organizational trust is based on a viable strategic plan that can be achieved, policies and practices that value all fairly, and the ability of leaders to demonstrate the competence to administer, implement and inspire both. Galford and Drapeau identified the essence of building organizational trust by identifying five variables on which organizational trust depends, as shown in the following equation:[13]

$$\text{Organizational Trust} = \frac{(A1 + A2 + A3) \times (A4 + A5)}{R}$$

where

A1 = Aspirations – aspirations provide the incentive for people in the organization to want to trust each other; a common goal the unit vision.

A2 = Abilities – the resources and capabilities required to fulfill the aspirations; competencies of individuals in the organization.

A3 = Actions – actually getting to the task and doing what is needed to reach the organizational goals rather than losing focus to the distractions that inevitably will arise; staying the course.

A4 = Alignment – having consistency between aspirations, abilities and actions; walking the talk.

A5 = Articulation – communicating the aspirations, abilities, actions, and alignment so that everybody in the organization knows them and is able to articulate them; must be a continuous effort.

R = Resistance – push back or hesitance in the form of skepticism, fear, frustration, and a "we-they" mindset.

Dancing On The Razor's EDGE

It is interesting that in the organizational trust formula, resistance is a common trait or characteristic of every single variable, and of the product of the sum of variables in the numerator. This realization will equip leaders with insight and hopefully a plan of action that directly addresses the issues behind the resistance of each variable. Leaders should understand that building organizational trust will take time, is a high-energy endeavor, and is a continuous process.

To help leaders recognize an environment of organizational trust I have listed some of the signs below.[14]

- Meetings after the meeting will be minimum.
- The same message from the top gets to the lowest person in the organization.
- Gossip is minimized.
- Communication and collaboration are real.
- Credit is shared.
- There is candor and authenticity.
- People feel empowered.
- People are not talked about negatively in their absence.
- There is a culture of innovativeness and mistakes are tolerated.

When one notices these behaviors in the interaction among the members of an organization, you can be assured that an environment of organizational trust is present. Organizational trust can be directly related to the ability to form new associations, and networks of trusting relationships within and across organizations to accomplish business transactions, and therefore, is a predictor of the viability of the organization (Fukuyama, 1995).[15] Also, overall employee job satisfaction, and perceived organizational effectiveness, have been the benefactors of trust (Money, Shockley-Zalabak, & Cesaria, 1997).[16] Consequently, trust is a fragile yet critical ingredient to the success of leadership, and the internal and external perceptions of the organization. As leaders, we must strive to not only build organizational trust, we must recognize when it is not present, as it is the change agent for transforming organizations.

Trust and Verify

Trust but Verify was a signature phrase of former President Ronald Reagan.[17] A new commander or leader of any organization would do well to adopt this behavior. I have modified the phrase somewhat to remove the exclusive conjunction of "but," and replaced it with "and," an inclusive conjunction. "The phrase "but," tends to convey a negation of "trust," however, "and" tends to convey an inclusion of "trust" and provides a positive spin on the act of verifying.[18] To practice it is a very delicate proposition depending on the situation or the individual that you are dealing with. On the behavior that supports it are somewhat diverging thoughts and actions. However, to verify is to prove the truth of, as by evidence, testimony, confirmation or substantiation.[19]

In organizational operations, a leader cannot, with good conscious, trust without verifying the information that is received. They must also verify that their directions were understood and carried out as expected. As a commander, I trusted the commitment of the individual to carry out an order based on established character and behavior. Additionally, I verified (the outcome/result) that what I directed was properly executed. In a fast moving environment, information about a situation can change in a heartbeat; thus, verification simply ensures that the information given has not changed since the last update.

This approach is a great mentoring tool for building accountability throughout the organization. I have often explained my position on "trust and verify" right up front, to preclude anyone from perceiving my actions in a negative or distrustful manner. In reality, the consistent behavior of trusting and verifying builds accountability into a person's actions and the outcome of the situation.

Establishing Trust Beyond the Organization

The building of trust had to be cultivated within our organization, as well as with other organizations and their leaders. It was critical to ensure that individuals and organizations that relied on us, or were potential customers, developed a positive perception of trustworthiness of our organization. As a business owner, I reflected on past business ventures where missed business opportunities were the result of not cultivating and leveraging a perception of organizational trust with other business owners. I was determined not to allow this to happen on my watch as a Commander, and pledged to diligently build confidence among other organizations and commanders. My desire was to build trust in my ability to command and in my unit's ability to deliver the right product, on time, the first time.

When I arrived at the unit, there was a perception of a lack of accountability, and a physical examination process issue that was eroding the unit's credibility. The accountability issue centered on airmen not returning to their units after receiving a physical in a timely manner. The process issue dealt with our attempt to address the perceptions of the lack of accountability. This perception presented undue, misdirected pressure on the medical unit to address accountability concerns that were not germane to administrating physicals and ensuring medically fit airmen. Our attempts to address this accountability disconnect diminished productivity by misuse of personnel and equipment. At that time, the examination process involved cycling individuals through two visits (two separate months) rather than finishing everything in one visit. In law, just as so many out dated laws are still on the books which were derived from dated circumstances, the current examination process of two visits was born out of facility constraints and mission requirements of the past. In addition, we were using valuable personnel to chaperone groups of patients to the different areas in the hospital where specific procedures were administered. This action was supposed to address the accountability of individuals and ensure everyone knew exactly where to go. This approach actually exacerbated the situation because not everyone in a group needed the same procedures, and this approach caused unnecessary bottlenecks in patient flow.

The process dilemma was a relatively easy fix after assessing the accommodation of physical and personnel resources. We had enough of both to complete a physical in one visit, which lessened the burden on everyone concerned. Seeing a doctor once vs. twice was easy to socialize throughout the Wing. Interesting ideas come forward when leaders ask for possible solutions rather than dictating them. One innovative airman drew up maps of the examination process to include floors, specific rooms, and phone numbers of the offices. Lesson learned; if you treat people like adults, most of the time, they will act the part. We respected individuals to get to their appointments without a chaperone, and expected them to return to duty once their examination was complete.

As the new Commander, I surmised that building organizational trust beyond the unit involved education, communication, motivation, and organizationally walking the talk. On the point of accountability, we educated, communicated and motivated Commanders, organizations, and individuals on new standard operating procedures (SOP) which placed accountability in its proper place given the process. This was instrumental in creating an atmosphere of cooperation and trust (internally and externally) in our process and the organization's effort. It also helped to identify the true violators of the process individually and organizationally.

A crucial piece of repairing our organizational trust was pinpointing where the breakdown of trust resided. Was it the individual, the scheduling organization, the medical organization, or a systematic process issue? At the point when we, as a wing, became congruent with both the process, and individual/organizational accountability, the act of trust became the foundation and the intersection by which organizational trust was built and sustained. Each organization then became a vested partner in the successful outcome of the mission.

Chapter 3 Leadership Takeaways

- Without trust, leadership is doomed to fail.

- The bottom line on how to gain the trust of those you lead, is to lead with **integrity**.

- Request time to prove your trustworthiness.

- Create an environment for success.

- Recognize organizational trust.

- Trust and verify.

- Establish trust beyond your organization.

****

**When you get what you want in your struggle of self
And the world makes you king for a day,
Just go to the mirror and look at yourself
And see what the man has to say.
For it isn't your father or mother or wife
Whose judgment upon you must pass.
The fellow whose verdict counts most in your life
Is the one staring back from the glass.**

****

"If you want one year of prosperity, grow grain,
If you want 10 years of prosperity, grow trees,
If you want 100 years of prosperity, grow people,"
Chinese proverb

Chapter 4

Followership

(To be a great leader you must first learn to be a great follower)

The sub-title of this section suggests that becoming a great leader is in part mastering the skill of being a great follower. Thinking of it another way, leadership and followership are two sides of the same coin.[20] Followership can be defined as a culture where people act with intelligence, independence, courage, and a strong sense of ethics. Additionally, a follower as one who shares a common purpose with the leader, believes in what the organization is trying to accomplish, and wants both the leader and the organization to succeed.

Effective followership skills, in contrast to just being a follower, are fundamental attributes that every leader should demonstrate in service of their organizations, and cultivate in those that they lead. "Jehn and Bezrukova suggested that good followers may be a catalyst for change in an organization as followership "inspires others to follow toward a common goal; creates enthusiasm and desire to excel; fully engages others; builds confidence; moves the organization ahead as one entity rather than separate parts."[21] That sounds like leadership also. Practicing LAP as a leader embodies the development of followership in those that you lead and mentor. To illustrate examples of leadership cultivating followership, I present two leaders who had a profound impact on developing followership in those that they influenced and inspired.

53

Great Mentors

I have had some great leaders to follow, learn from, and serve with. Great leaders see the potential in those they lead, even beyond what a person may see in him or herself. I have been blessed with two such leaders in Colonel Roger Wujek, (Retired), and Colonel Ivan Lee Craft, now deceased. Both saw the potential in me and took the time and energy to mentor me through mistake after mistake, and I owe each a huge amount of gratitude and respect for taking me under their wing.

Colonel Roger Wujek

Colonel Wujek is a highly successful medical doctor with his own practice in Litchfield, Illinois, and was the commander of the 932nd Aeromedical Staging Squadron (ASTS) at Scott AFB Illinois. I tutored under Colonel Wujek's leadership as a new Major through the rank of Lieutenant Colonel, as his administrator/executive officer, and later as his deputy group commander when he became the group commander of three large medical units. He was a visionary leader and tactician who led through motivation and care for his people. He also had the gift of the power of the pen, which he used to create a new medical mission for the Air Force that made medical operations more viable for the wars of the future.

One particular incident that Colonel Wujek resolved, helped me see the measure of a leader that he is, in building lasting relationships that fosters followership. Unfortunately, one of the personnel in the unit received a Driving Under the Influence (DUI), during a gate check, while entering the base. When this happens to an airman, he or she is detained, and the Commander is immediately notified of the incident. In order to be released from confinement, the Commander must sign for the individual to be remitted to his custody.

This was a very embarrassing situation for the individual as well as the organization, and it has to be reported to superiors. The individual in this case was upstanding, a hard worker, intelligent, and had the makings of a great leader. This incident was the first and only infraction of judgment that I noted in this person for as long as I knew them.

Given the rank of the person, Colonel Wujek could have justifiably taken a number of measures that would have in effect ended the person's Air Force career. How he handled the situation was with a measure of dignity, discernment, compassion, and leadership that is only displayed from great leaders. He took into account the character, potential, and humility of the individual in making his decision about what course of action to take. He surmised that this incident was out of character, and a lapse of judgment. Understanding the gravity of the situation, his actions were measured, yet stern and judicious. He administered appropriate disciplinary actions that acknowledged the significance of the infraction without destroying the career of the airman.

His actions showed that he was a take-charge leader with uncompromising values, which sent a clear message for all to follow. The justness of his actions also served to build trust in his judgment throughout the organization. Trust is a fundamental ingredient for building exemplary followership. The airman understood the trust that was bestowed from Colonel Wujek on a future of uncompromised performance as an Air Force member. That understanding and dedication to duty transformed the airman, who successfully completed a Doctoral degree program and became an exceptional leader. From Colonel Wujek, I learned leadership through humility (being proud to serve), as he was ever mindful of his responsibility to the mission and to the care of his airmen. He is a true patriot and servant leader.

Dancing On The Razor's EDGE

Colonel Ivan Lee Craft

Of equal influence in my life was Colonel Ivan Craft, former Medical Director of the Health Services Management Division at 4th Air Force, March ARB, California. Colonel Craft died suddenly on 21 March, 2007. Colonel Craft was a leader who possessed the uncanny ability to not only see one's potential, but to project them into positions that provided genuine growth for the individual as well as for the entire organization. Great leaders listen. Colonel Craft was very good at listening to his followers and directing their energies to find the leader within. To his credit, I was pulled reluctantly to greater responsibilities as the Medical Director Health Services Management Branch at 4th Air Force. Colonel Craft knew that I needed to see and experience a bigger picture of the Air Force Reserves if I was to contribute on a larger scale as a future leader. He understood the dynamics of growing a leader; helping them to broaden their perspective, develop a vision, and build a solid platform from which to lead. He not only did this for me, but for countless others who are now great leaders themselves.

One of his duties at 4th Air Force was chief of the staff assistance teams that visited units within 4th Air Force to ensure their compliance with stated regulations and policies established to successfully manage and lead medical organizations. Medical organizations viewed staff assistance visits (SAV) as a rehearsal for their upcoming Health Service Inspection. Having been a member of the SAV team with Colonel Craft was an enriching experience of leadership in action. He had the ability to take the most difficult situations that we encountered and turn them into positive, motivating experiences that uplifted organizations and individuals. He had the ability to see through any challenge for the ultimate opportunity that it presented. Colonel Craft did not waiver in calling the situation as he saw it, good or bad, but he would also offer solutions for the way forward and seized the opportunity to mentor junior and senior airmen. His passion was mentoring and growing individuals to be the best leaders that they could possibly be. By doing so, he cultivated followership (leadership, accountability, and professionalism) in everyone that he encountered.

When we meet leaders of this caliber, a gradual transformation takes place in one's ability to lead on all fronts. In most leadership situations, I often find myself asking the question, what would they do? Then I find the way. A large measure of any leadership successes that I have experienced have been directly attributable to the followership and leadership experiences shared by, and with, these two great men.

Developing Followership

Leaders are not leaders without followers. Therefore, two questions should be answered when examining leader/follower relationships. Why are they following, and what type of followers are we leading? Answering these questions, will expose understanding that supports the development of followership in those we lead. Followers choose to follow out of fear, blind hope, faith in their leader, intellectual agreement (mental connection), and belief in the vision (inspired connection).[22] The type of follower is closely connected to the reason for following. The range of types of followers spans from passive to dynamic, and ultimately exemplary.

The passive follower is aligned with reasons of fear or blind hope submissively supporting whatever the leader proposes. The dynamic follower in contrast, is actively engaged and self-motivated based on faith in the leader, and/or intellectual agreement. The exemplary follower's all-consuming dedication is based on an inspired connection with the vision. An exemplary follower is empowered, and makes a body, mind, soul, spirit commitment to work passionately in achieving the organization's goals.

In layman's terms, creating followership is simply genuinely caring about the people you are entrusted to lead. The people we lead are our most valuable commodity, and leading them should never be taken lightly. Valuing followers and their development are the first steps toward cultivating effective transformational leaders; people capable of motivating followers to achieve mission requirements in the absence of immediate or visible rewards.[23] Followers choose whom they wish to follow, and whom they empower through that action.[24]

A leader's dynamic leadership/followership efforts should produce individuals who seamlessly transition to lead effectively when the moment arrives, while simultaneously fulfilling their follower roles in support of their superiors.[25] As leaders develop exemplary followership in those they lead, their followers will in turn develop competencies necessary to achieve the visions articulated by the leader for mission effectiveness.[26]

Strategies for cultivating emempliary followership suggest that leaders focus on two areas: performance and relationships.[27] Within these two categories are competency subsets that, when mastered, create partnership in the leader/follower relationship that is only distingishable by rank or position. Performance involves working effectively with others, embracing change, producing competently, and valuing oneself as an asset/investment to the organization.[28]

Relationship involves building trust, connecting with the leader, embracing the leader's vision, and communicating audaciously.[29] While performance deals with efforts related to organizational team building, relationship focuses on the one-on-one by one-at-a-time relationship building between leaders and followers of a shared responsibility for an effective relationship. The mutual benefit of becoming highly proficient in both areas yields a leader/follower environment where the probability is maximized for the speed with which visions are realized and organizational success is accomplished.

Effective leaders know that their point of view influences their subordinates. Therefore, what is important/unimportant to the leader becomes important/unimportant to followers. What is peramount, is that followers clearly understand the leader's message and expectations. Establishing avenues of communication that support the leaders' vision, values and expections is critical to both leadership and followership. By developing followership in those you lead, the most important contribution leaders make to their organizations is asssured--that the mission can continue without them.[30]

Developing followership in the 459th AMDS encompassed a multitude of leader/follower initiatives. In the relationship arena we suffered the lack of bold open communication avenues that supported what was important to leadership and what was necessary for accomplishment of vision/mission objectives. It was critical to establish this relationship to support our quest to turn our situation around. Particularly, the leadership message was not always getting to the newest or lowest ranking persons in the organization with the intensity or the actual meaning of the original message. We knew this situation existed because we tested it by making an effort to talk to the newest or lowest ranking person in the organization from time to time. More profound than the validation of our perceptions was the airman's reaction to our efforts to actually seek them out, and value their opinion in my quest for mission success.

Developing followership means followers must hear your message the way it was intended from the top of the organization to the bottom. Anything less will prove ineffective and possibly damaging. The concept and practice of LAP was intented to be at the forefront of everyone's mind, and most importantly the newest person. We wanted to indoctrinate them on the culture that was being established so that no time was wasted in gaining their support for accomplishing the mission. New members were usually recognized and asked to introduce themselves during our first meeting of the weekend. At that time, they were told how proud we were to have them on board, and by the next month they were expected to know the meaning of LAP. Each supervisor knew that part of in-processing an individual into their section involved explaining LAP, and the expected behavior with respect to practicing LAP.

At one of our meetings, I had the opportunity to ask a newcomer what the meaning of LAP was, and to my surprise, she did not know. It was interesting what happened next, and it happens when an idea, movement, or culture is born and supported. It does not take the leader to express direct discontent with noncompliance because the followers will express their own sense of disappointment. When the airman said she did not know the meaning of LAP, the entire unit uninformly sighed, just as a crowd does when a golfer misses a putt in the game of golf. At that point, being very careful not to shun the new person publicly (as it was not her fault), I only said we are sure you will know it the next time you are asked. Immediately after the meeting, that individual's supervisor came up to me and apologized for not making sure that his airman got the message. In fact, before the end of that day, that particular supervisor had put together a power point presentation on the practice of LAP for his airman. His efforts went far above the call of duty and from that day forward his power point presentation was shared with other newcomers when introducing the practice of LAP. You can bet that the next time that airman was asked, she surely knew the meaning of LAP and more.

The situation that I just shared is one aspect of developing followership by communicating the expectations and values of the leader through the members of the organization who are themselves leaders and followers. Communication is the key to both leadership and followership relationships. Developing exemplary followership in those you lead, and embracing them as partners, means sharing information, co-creating the vision and mission statements, and shared risks and rewards.[31] The principles of LAP, leadership, accountability, and professionalism are the tenets of a practice that cultivated an atmosphere of exemplary followership, and transformed followers into self-motivated, self-directed leaders who connected with the leader within.

Chapter 4 Leadership Takeaways

- Great leaders must first learn to follow.

- Find your mentor and follow him or her.

- Do not be afraid to make mistakes.

- Listen and take all constructive criticism to heart.

- Be reflective and see the real you in the mirror.

- Leadership and followership are reciprocal in nature.

- Dynamic leadership creates dynamic followers.

- Dynamic followers are the essence of mission success.

"The greatest good is not that which renders one dependent,
Instead, it is that which transforms dependence into independence"
Arthur R. Nicholson

Chapter 5

Making the Tough Calls

L eaders in every level of an organization will at some point have to make hard, and sometimes gut wrenching decisions. The quote at the beginning of this chapter is relevant here because leaders making the tough calls may have to act with an independent mind to take the right course of action. Nothing in particular prepares you for this aspect of leadership, except knowing that it will come, facing the fact that a decision must be made, and the experience of doing so. I am sharing the following stories because they taught me some valuable lessons that have helped me in my leadership role as commander when I had to make the tough calls.

I was in pilot training at Williams AFB in Phoenix, AZ, the land of sunshine and good times for a young student pilot. Williams AFB was considered one of the best pilot training bases to learn to fly simply because of the consistently great weather. My dream was to fly the white rocket, the T-38 super sonic aircraft used in advanced flight training at the time. The T-38 was a very sleek and sexy two-engine, tandem seated aircraft that seemed to slice through the air without any regard to nature's pull of gravity or man's manufactured components of drag (shape of aircraft). I wanted to fly this aircraft more than anything else in the world, and I did. This aircraft was about speed and nothing else, as you took off in afterburner and landed with almost as much speed. I had no problem taking off or landing the T-38, and I have been told that landing such an aircraft with its very short wingspan is one of the most difficult aircraft to land. However, I did encounter significant challenges executing designated flight profiles (acrobatic maneuvers back to back) within my designated area of flight, sufficient to sustain my status in pilot training.

Flying a high performance aircraft is all about keeping the energy level sufficiently high enough to perform a set of maneuvers. Ironically, leadership involves that same concept; keeping the energy level high to execute the mission. Based on my performance, my evaluators assessed that I could not finish pilot training within the time line designated for my class. Washing (placing) me back to a lower class was not an option at the time; therefore, I was eliminated from Undergraduate Pilot Training (UPT). Someone in a leadership role ultimately made that decision. The leadership lesson here, is how that decision was communicated to me given the huge disappointment that was sure to follow. Needless to say, I was completely devastated, as I had said to myself many times, if I can finish UPT, I can do anything. If you have ever wanted something to happen more than anything else in your life, and it did not, you know how I was feeling at that time. Although I qualified as a private pilot before entering UPT, my ultimate goal was to become an Air Force pilot and I had failed.

I am not sure that I can explain the hurt and dejection that I felt within for years to come. The hurt was so profound because I truly knew inside that I did not give it my all. I have often asked myself how I would ever use the devastation, humiliation, and rejection of that experience in any part of my life going forward. I share this story because we as leaders may have to make like decisions that may be devastating to someone. Sometimes it is not making the call that is the hardest; it is executing it in a manner that causes the least amount of collateral damage on the individual or the situation. It is here that the professionalism of a leader plays an important role. It is not so much about what you do, but how you do it (compassion).

The next example is ultimately about tough love leadership. It is a story born out of love, desiring better, knowing that better exists, and ultimately making the tough call. Although the story is about what occurred to my sister and me, it is ultimately about one of the toughest calls that my parents had to make regarding their children. In 1956, the year of my birth, the school systems in Tennessee were desegregated, which meant that whites could attend black schools and blacks could attend white schools. The former (whites choosing to attend black schools) was a rare occasion, if ever, but in time blacks either chose or were forced to attend white schools because of black school closings. My mother made the choice (ahead of being forced) when I was entering the third grade and my sister was entering first grade, to send my sister and me to the all white school system.

The year was 1964, 8 years after desegregation in Tennessee was legalized. You would think that after the passing of the law, and 8 years hence, that making such a decision would not be a big deal. But it was! The reality is passing of a law does not produce an immediate cultural change in any of the cultures targeted by the law. In 1962 and 1963 I attended an all black school that served the first through the sixth grades. The school was approximately an hour and a half from our home, which meant my school day for my first two years spanned over 14 hours. Most black students during that time experienced the same given, that their schools were not in their neighborhoods.

My mother's decision was made solely on the longevity of our school day and its impact on our quality of life; not on the quality of schooling and guidance received from the black school system. In fact, she always supplemented our school teachings with ample amounts of home instruction. Going to the white school which was in our community decreased our school day by about 3 hours. As the one going through that experience, I was not convinced that a shorter school day and the humiliation that I experienced was worth it all, or equated to a better quality of life. Without going through any specific experiences, I will say that it was a very frightening experience initially, for an eight year old riding the bus with all whites, some much older, and being in class with peers who did not know what to think of you, and others who down right hated you for even being in their space.

Getting back to the leadership part of this story, my mother and father must have analyzed, agonized, and prayed over their decision many times before making it and following through. This is an example of making the tough call, in the face of some very extenuating circumstances, that involved and affected individuals (the children) who did not have the advantage of fully understanding the implications of the decision. Growing through this experience, and later understanding the gravity of the situation in which their decision was made, has given me a genuine appreciation for the leadership that they displayed. They had to be independent of thought and deed as their decision was made, in the face of overwhelming peer opposition (concern for the children), and the wave of humiliation and dejection actually experienced by their children. Thank GOD for my parents.

A thick face, black heart approach

Leaders, sometimes have to put on the thick face and execute in a black heart manner that which is the right thing to do for the good of the mission and for the good of the individual.

My realization of this concept of leadership came after reading a book entitled "Thick Face Black Heart" by Chin-Ning Chu.[32] Thick Face Black Heart is a concept and which when implemented, governs successful behavior in every aspect of life and forges a path to thriving, winning, and succeeding.

With the passing of time and the benefit of hind site, my flight training and integration experiences helped me realize that leaders must develop the tool of a thick face, black heart. Effective leaders, who are connected to the leader within, are more qualified and well equipped to handle these most delicate situations. Being qualified means that one has faced a delicate situation that required a tough decision. Being well equipped means that one has developed a situational leadership tool set to use in making the tough call and executing it. I know that my parents were qualified and had an expanded tool set to choose from. The most troubling decisions are those that, on the face of it (looking from outside in), say you do not care (thick face, black heart).

Leaders who make these tough calls, yet preserve the dignity of the person, gain the trust and admiration of the people that they lead. I, too, have had to tell airmen that they could no longer be a part of the organization, and to my surprise, I have been thanked by the very individual that was being dismissed. One young airman that I had to dismiss told me that she was not particularly good with handling failure, and if allowed to continue she surely would have failed. She also stated that another failure would have been devastating to her well being and future.

In pilot training, a leader had to make the thick face, black heart call that temporally stopped my clock. I was in a very fragile state of mind at that time, because I wanted to complete undergraduate pilot training so badly and had expended so much energy getting there. It is absolutely critical that we as leaders understand that our charge is to preserve the one-ounce of dignity that a person needs in order to continue, and recover from such a failure. Fortunately, the individual that shared my fate with me understood the gravity of the moment and lived up to his charge as a compassionate leader. With my one-ounce of dignity preserved, I have continued to grow beyond that failure, to strive for excellence in other areas of my life. I learned from that experience, and was able to use the lessons learned to do the same in a very compassionate way for others. I learned how to preserve the spirit and will of the individual so that they could regroup, refocus, and know that a particular failure should not define in total the outcome of the rest of one's life.

Professionalism and Making the Tough Call

This is an area where professionalism in practicing LAP pays maximum benefits. Professionalism here is not just knowing what decision to make, it is executing that decision swiftly, judiciously, and with a certain amount of compassion. The thick face, black heart approach and professionalism are two sides of the same coin. The professionalism demonstrated in the execution of a thick face, black heart decision tempers the situation and preserves the dignity of the individual. When leaders prolong the inevitable decision without cause, distrust, lack of confidence, misdirection, and confusion are the by products of such action. Just the opposite occurs when tough decisions are made timely, in line with goals and objectives, and the leader has applied due diligence in the decision process. Trust is preserved, confidence in leadership solidifies, and followership increases to another level knowing that their leader will stand in the gap and make the call that is beneficial to the mission and to the people.

Chapter 5 Leadership Takeaways

- Leaders of organizations will have to make hard and sometimes gut wrenching decisions.

- The failure of one dream is not the end of all dreams.

- The lessons learned from failure are the wisdom of future success.

- Life is rich with thick face, black heart decisions.

- Know that failure should not define in total the outcome of the rest of one's life.

- The thick face, black heart approach and professionalism are two sides of the same coin.

****

**Sheep led by a lion
would defeat
lions led by a sheep.
~Arab Proverb~**

****

"One should strive to stay in balance with one's surroundings not being so small minded as to have no peripheral vision and not being so worldly that all things are seen in a blur"

Arthur R. Nicholson

Chapter 6

The Mission

The 459th Aerospace Medicine Squadron's number one mission is to provide medical support for the Wing assuring medical deployment readiness of each member. However, at this point, we were broken, and it was our job to roll up our sleeves and figure out exactly how broken we were. We desperately needed to lead the way if we were to realize our vision and accomplish the mission. Believe me, that was much easier said than done. Rising from broken to benchmark involved assembling a top-notch team to make it all happen. We did just that in the following manner.

Understanding the Mission

Before we could gain an understanding of our mission, we had to define our mission to meet the challenges we faced as a unit. Our official mission statement addressed the following:

o Provide medical support for the Wing to assure deployment readiness.
o Provide personnel and trained medical staff for Air force and joint contingencies and/or humanitarian missions.
o Provide professional growth and leadership opportunities to all unit members.
o Provide an improved quality of life for our internal customers.

When a leader takes control of an organization that is broken, he or she must identify where the break is with regard to process, personnel and/or both. In our case it was both, which compounded the energy necessary to correct the course. Leaders will have to correct course and refine their focus many times as they push the agenda of their chief concern, successful mission accomplishment. Mission accomplishment is first about an in-depth understanding of the mission in light of personnel, equipment, facilities, and funding requirements. A good leader will take a deep dive into understanding what the mission is (internal and external impacts) before attempting to execute it. After gaining this knowledge, they must understand who they will interface with to accomplish the mission.

It is most helpful to establish a working relationship on a first name, face-to-face basis if possible. There will inevitably be times that having established that relationship will prove most helpful in getting things done in an expeditious manner, without all of the red tape. In the last days leading up to the Health Services Inspection, having established these relationships paid maximum dividends in gaining funding, manpower, and facility support in an expeditious manner.

Understanding Leadership Limitations

Whether you are a leader of a small office or a large multi-level organization, one thing remains constant, and that is you cannot do it all by yourself. In my situation, it was very clear to me that I was the leader of a very talented and diverse group of doctors, nurses, medical technicians, and a host of other professionals that I needed to work with to get the job done. When you realize that you cannot be a one-man band, (Tiger Woods, Venus and Serena Williams,

Michael Phelps) you must develop the art of leadership. Being a one-man band means that one can accomplish everything that needs to be done, without relying on the efforts of anyone else. The art of leadership is the ability to influence/inspire others to get the job done despite the leader's lack of specialized knowledge or the volume of the task. Leaders have to know what needs to be done, but not necessarily how to do it. My job as I saw it, was being a servant leader, and influencing the process by providing whatever the organization needed to meet its stated goals.

Choosing an Executive Committee

The establishment and development of a solid and effective Executive Committee was one of the first actions I accomplished soon after my arrival at the 459th AMDS. After our first few meetings it became obvious to me that this working group needed a major overhaul. There were issues of proper representation, preparation, expectation, validation, and punctuality that needed to be addressed. As the senior leader, I had to share my expectations with this leader group, firmly holding them accountable and responsible. I knew that if I could not lead this group and implement the practice of LAP among them, the vision and the mission were doomed.

It is critical that a leader understand the importance of an organization's executive committee. The executive committee is to the organization just as the brain is to the body. Without the executive committee, the organization will soon lose direction just as the body will lose direction without a brain and in both cases, death may occur. The 459th AMDS's executive committee consisted of representatives from every major functional area and/or major program area. It was charged to propose/implement the unit's strategy and policies, draft budgets, review/approve reports and provide executive leadership. Understanding the value of an effective executive committee and the egos that sometimes come with this leader group, helped me develop a saying that I used from time to time that addressed value versus privilege. "We all have some measure of value, but none of us are privileged." Reciting my value statement came in handy as a reality check to the executive committee and to the unit. Additionally, to help this committee stay grounded and focused, I imposed the expectation that the executive committee would be a group of servant leaders to the organization. The newly formed executive committee in time became a highly effective group that graduated from a reactive mode of operation to a perceptive and proactive servant leadership group.

Developing a Strategic Plan

A strategic plan determines where an organization is going over the next 3-5 years, how it is going to get there, and how the organization will know when it gets there. The focus of a strategic plan is usually on the entire organization. The 459th AMDS had not operated with an up-to-date strategic plan for several years, and was working in reactive mode. Defining what the mission was, who the players were, and where we were broken, was the basis of developing a strategic plan of attack to achieve a benchmark status. Although, most strategic plans cover up to five years, I suggested to our executive committee that our plan not exceed three years. This approach would ensure that we were focused on the mission. I knew that I had set the bar high with the vision that was laid out. However, I did not want to overwhelm the organization by looking ahead five years when they at this point, did not understand the vision for the next 16 months.

I did not have to look very far to find someone to lead the charge in developing the strategic plan. Major Thomas

Connelly was the unit Administrator, and I noticed that he had an enormous amount of untapped capacity to contribute to the cause. Major Connelly was an U.S. Air Force Academy graduate, with extensive hospital executive training from time served on active duty; and he was rapidly climbing the executive ladder as a civilian.

One important aspect of leadership is understanding the capacity of the individuals that answer directly to you. Taking the time to know the strengths and challenges of your people pays dividends in three very positive ways. First, you are more likely to place the right person in the right job at the right time. Second, you are better equipped to affect the development of the individual to his or her fullest potential; and third, the mission is accomplished in a more efficient/effective manner.

Major Connelly definitely represented the tip of the spear of the executive committee and took the lead in revising the strategic plan to meet our new vision, mission, and unit goals. As with everything that had to be accomplished prior to the inspection, the development of the strategic plan required maximum effort. We utilized various forms of meeting and communication, to include telephone meetings, in developing the plan. It was amazing how with a little direction, the executive committee members were feeding off of each other's energy and enthusiasm in the development of the strategic plan. The typical forming, storming, and norming phases of such functions was minimal and the strategic plan was developed in record time. To my amazement, the strategic plan had each executive team member's complete support. As a leader, it was a pleasure and joy to work with a truly dedicated team of servant leaders. Their efforts served to lay a solid foundation for building a benchmark organization.

When the leader and the executive team are working well, the entire organization will be firing on all cylinders in a proactive and visionary manner. As with any plan, for buy-in, our plan had to be presented and promoted to the entire organization. Major Connelly and I presented the strategic plan to the entire organization, however, clarifying each person's role, providing encouragement, and reinforcing action took the entire executive team. The successful execution of our strategic plan was directly attributable to Major Connelly and the executive team for their continuous effort to create buy-in, accountability, and ensure that everyone understood their part in the plan.

Socializing the Vision, Mission and Strategic Plan

Socializing here means to familiarize, gather feedback, foster consensus, and build ownership. Continuously restating the vision, mission, and strategic plan was necessary to preclude any setbacks or temporary lack of confidence. The seed of doubt can grow like a weed in the midst of the most solid plan. Sometimes the leader will be the only cheerleader. It is at this point, that leaders must reenergize the base (executive committee) to stay the course, and reassure them of your commitment to stay on point. It is not magic, but it feels that way when you get a few believing in themselves and the vision. The confidence builds, and becomes infectious for the entire organization. We preached that being a part of something great took commitment that exceeded the norm. The vision, mission, and strategic plan were born out of a commitment to excellence, nurtured with sacrifice, focus, and continuous socialization to solidify their successful completion.

Internal/External Feedback Approach

Our feedback approach involved continuously assessing our progress internally and externally from all points: North, South, East and West of the organization. When I arrived at the unit, it was obvious that we had some internal issues and processes to repair. It was also apparent through my associations with higher headquarters, that we had a real credibility issue to deal with, which meant that we had to address external perceptions. When we developed our strategic plan, we built in objectives and approaches that addressed both of these concerns simultaneously. Getting feedback from all points, meant engaging on all levels (North-leaders, South-subordinates, East/West-peers) internal, and external to the organization, to gauge progress, gain perspective, and assess perceptions. This process proved very valuable in validating mission accomplishment with all of our customers in mind. At any given time, based on an established and fluid feedback network, we knew where to apply effort to correct a process, educate, or perform damage control to avoid escalation of a situation.

Making Decisions on Evidenced Based Results

Making decisions on the most timely/accurate data available is the surest approach to predictable success. As we were digging out of the hole of failure, we received a plethora of advice about how to make things better. Although each suggestion was sincere with intent to improve our plight, it was difficult to know which practice to implement to get a desired result. Deciding which advice or direction to take was compounded by having to address multiple challenges simultaneously. At this point in our recovery, we were in reaction mode, responding to situations without empirical data, to make intelligent decisions about possible courses of actions.

A leader's situational awareness gained from an evidence-based decision yields a foundation from which to advocate more effectively for a decided course of action.[33] Accordingly, an evidence based decision-making process provides a more rational, credible basis for the decisions made, and is built on objective evidence, which is difficult to neutralize.[34] Ultimately, objective evidence elevates the discussion, and helps to professionalize the discussion. A leader's charge is to determine which direction to go based on analyzing the most accurate data available that supports an immediate decision or the distant vision.

Making decisions on evidence-based results is an approach that integrates strategy, people, resources, processes, and measurements to improve decision-making, transparency, and accountability.[35] The objectives of this approach are to achieve outcomes, learn while responding to change, implement performance measurement, and accurately report performance.[36] In a process-orientated environment such as physical examination, evidence (data) and results tell a story, and we, as leaders must pay attention to such data if we are to be successful in making improvements to the process.

In January 2007, it was apparent that we were not paying attention to the evidence or metrics to make an educated decision about which course of action to take, or even why the existing one failed. For example, the 459th AMDS was being charged with a lack of accountability in its physical examination process because it appeared that the process was taking an entire day for everyone to complete. In some instances that was true, but for 75 percent of the physicals, four hours or less was sufficient. To answer this charge, we were grouping patients and leading them to each examination areas in an effort to ensure accountability of the process and individual.

This approach was problematic on several levels. It produced inefficiencies into the process by utilizing valuable personnel as needless chaperones, masked individual and process accountability, and lengthened the process for everyone involved. This approach was clearly reactionary based, and was not supported by any available data. However, analyzing the data revealed that a short physical only took four hours maximum. With that data and records of individual's completion times, we educated Commanders and placed accountability exactly where it needed to be, on the individual. We discontinued chaperones and replaced them with maps of the physical examination process to include floors, room numbers and points of contact. This action freed up needed personnel to support other operational and administrative functions. Our data based course of action also allowed for better quality control implementation of the examination process.

Leaders will have individuals in their organization who are analytical by nature; use them. The person that I most relied on in this area was Master Sergeant (MSgt) Edward Thomas (now First Lieutenant) who was the right person to be in charge of the organization's self-inspection program because his approach was evidence-based. As the leader, you should be able to look very quickly at a set of metrics that will tell you if the organization is succeeding or failing at the mission. Analyzing a marginal or failing metric is just as important as analyzing a high performing metric. Careful study of a metric can reveal the nature of a trend in order to eliminate or replicate the process in other areas of the organization, if applicable. With MSgt Thomas' insight, we were able to target our resources to affect predictable outcomes/results. These evidence-based results further assisted leadership decisions, and our efforts became metrics based from top to bottom, which directly contributed to our mission success.

Flexibility

Sir Basil H. Liddel-Hart stated, "Only by this flexibility of aim can strategy be attuned to the uncertainty of war."[37] Flexibility is the key to sustainability in an ever-changing environment and accomplishing any mission. In a Wing, just as in any large organization, your mission is just one of many that are taking place simultaneously. Recognizing this point is also realizing competing points of view, and prioritization of resources to accomplish the mission. The challenges of accomplishing your specific mission can be frustrating as a leader, and practicing flexibility is the mechanism by which to overcome the frustration.

Flexibility allows for creativity in search for the win/win solution. Leaders should be ever conscious of the mistake of imposing the "my way or the highway approach" in all situations. Inflexibility carries with it a small toolbox from which to operate and build. In contrast, flexibility allows for inclusiveness, buy-in, and accountability in the decision making process and grows the toolbox. Leaders at various stages of their careers need to be flexible enough to expand their toolboxes and reorganize them to make sure that they are using the right leadership tools that will produce the intended outcome.

Tip of the Spear Existence

A leader, setting the pace, leading by example, and staying out front takes a tremendous amount of focus and energy. Yet leaders must do just that, to crystallize the vision and accomplish the mission. Being the first in and the last out says a lot, but your efforts cannot be just a show. There has to be genuineness and substance in your presence as a servant leader. One cannot simply show up, blow up, and leave others to clean up. We have all known those type of leaders who show up just at the right time to get the credit, blow up at the right time to get the attention, and leave at the right time to avoid any accountability for the broken glass left in their wake that others have to clean up. That is not the tip of the spear existence of servant leadership.

Servant leaders show up before the cameras or any hint of credit given. They run interference and blow up their followers for their sacrifice and duty to the mission. Lastly, these leaders stay to the end accepting all accountability for outcomes. If there is any broken glass to clean up, you can count on them to do so. The by-product of consistent actions of a leader living the tip of the spear existence, is that people begin to know that they can count on one's behavior (trust).

A leader's actions become his expected behavior, it precedes him in the form of a reputation, and follows him in the form of a legacy. Setting the example cannot be just for the cameras, because frankly, when the cameras are off everyone else is still watching. When I was a Deputy Group Commander, I got a wake up call that hit me squarely between the eyes. I was giving a young officer a ride and during the conversation, he said, "Sir, I just want to thank you for walking the talk." In his mind, he meant that I practice what I preach. In addition, he said others that he associated with were saying the same.

What struck me was not that he and others had observed the congruence in my behavior with my speech; it was that so many were watching and taking note. I have shared this story with leaders that I have mentored, and informed them that as you ascend the leadership ladder, the platform from which to operate becomes broader and the margin for error becomes narrower. Therefore, if your actions, which are tagged as example setting, are not a real part of who you are, they will be perceived as inconsistent, shallow, self-serving, and only for the cameras.

I urge those I mentor to take stock in why they desire to be out front, and to make sure that it is for the right reasons; ultimately, servant leadership is about taking care of people who take care of the mission. Staying out front as a leader is about two things, providing guidance, and running interference for those you lead. When a leader's followers trust him, have confidence in his ability, and support his vision, it is a comforting and calming feeling to have that leader as the tip of their spear. As leaders, we must strive to achieve this level of trust in our organizations. Great leadership lives on the tip of the spear existence, which begets trust, accountability, and performance. Mix that with a healthy dose of professionalism and you have a formula for mission accomplishment and continued success.

Chapter 6 Leadership Takeaways

- A leader will have to correct course and refine their focus many times, as he or she drives toward successful mission accomplishment.

- The executive committee is to the organization just as the brain is to the body.

- We all have some measure of value, but none of us are privileged.

- Leadership is understanding the capacity of individuals, in order to affect their development to the fullest potential.

- The seed of doubt can grow like a weed in the midst of the most solid plan.

- Flexibility is the key to sustainability in an ever-changing environment and allows for creativity in search of the win/win solution.

- A leader's actions become his expected behavior, it precedes him in the form of a reputation, and follows him in the form of a legacy.

- Great leadership lives on the tip of the spear existence, which begets trust, accountability, and performance.

Pictures of Some of the Leaders who Danced on the Razors EDGE

They are a Part of Something Great

****

"Realizing all there is in you gives life to all there is of you."

~ ARN ~

****

Colonel Stacey Harris (now Brigadier General)
at her Change of Command

04/01/2007

Colonel Roger Wujek (Retired) and I at my
promotion (Col) ceremony

Colonel Ivan Craft and I at my going away party
(4th AF RMG, March ARB, CA)

4th AF medical crew and friends
(4th AF RMG, March ARB, CA)

Colonel George Cohen reviewing a medical record, 459th AMDS, AFB, MD

04/14/2007

Maj. Connelly instructing a class at the 459th AMDS, Andrews AFB MD

Me as Commander of the Troops (wing) the moment just before rendering the final salute to Brigadier General Harris

The wing rendering final salute to Brigadier General Harris

*"Dreams are that which is between thoughts and action
Thus, dreams realized are the result of thought processes put into action"*

Arthur R. Nicholson

Chapter 7

The Committed Few
vs.
The Uncommitted Many

"The committed few" is a concept that captures and labels the commitment and effort of those few who can always be counted on to give their best. Howard Thurman said, "Commitment means that it is possible for a man to yield the nerve center of his consent to a purpose or cause, a movement or an ideal, which may be more important to him than whether he lives or dies."[38] In addition, Tom Flores said, "A total commitment is paramount to reaching the ultimate in performance."[39]

When the concept of the "committed few" was introduced to the unit members, I told them that we could do more with the committed few than with a multitude of uncommitted many. The dynamics of the phrase itself are very interesting. When most people think of commitment, they refer to yester years when people worked for one company a lifetime or stayed married to the same person for life. I agree, but in these changing times, I view the essence of commitment unchanged when associated with a task or mission completion irrespective of time. In other words, I think one can be committed to a mission that lasts one week, or one that lasts one year. It is not the time spent, as much as it is the concentration and expression of effort to the cause, i.e. commitment. "The quality of a person's life is in direct proportion to their commitment to excellence, regardless of their chosen field of endeavor." (Vince Lombardi)[40]

Pareto's Principle

The other aspect to examine in the phrase "the committed few" is the few versus the many. The 80/20 rule comes into play here. In 1906, Italian economist Vilfredo Pareto created a mathematical formula to describe the unequal distribution of wealth in his country, observing that twenty percent of the people owned eighty percent of the wealth.[41] "Quality Management pioneer, Dr. Joseph Juran, working in the US in the 1930s and 40s recognized a universal principle he called the "vital few and trivial many" and reduced it to writing."[42] As a result, Dr. Juran's observation of the "vital few and trivial many," the principle that 20 percent of something always are responsible for 80 percent of the results, became known as Pareto's Principle or the 80/20 Rule. The 80/20 Rule means that in anything, a few are vital and many are trivial. "You can apply the 80/20 Rule to almost anything, from the science of management to the physical world, but it is most often applied to businesses."[43]

Long Tail Theory

In contrast, the Long Tail Theory is a concept that somewhat counters the golden 80/20 Rule. The phrase the Long Tail was first coined by Chris Anderson in an October 2004 "Wired" magazine article to describe the niche strategy of businesses, that sell a large number of unique items, each in relatively small quantities. The Long Tail Theory is derived from Pareto's thinking that low demand can effectively and collectively make up a market share that exceeds the few of those that are in high demand. What this means is that in aggregate, all the small customers exceed in volume that of the popular volume. In the Long Tail phenomenon, the trivial in-mass out-perform the vital, making the vital insignificant and the insignificant vital. In other words, a large number of small customers can potentially out-perform a small number of large customers.[44]

My Theory

I subscribed to both theories and utilized them to get the mission accomplished. I initially recognized that only a few would understand and accept my vision for several reasons. Introducing change (the vision) also introduces risk that some are not be willing to take, others are comfortable with the status quo, and still others will not think it achievable. Leaders should embrace the fact that you may start with a vision that only you believe in, and not the 20 percent.

Ultimately, to get the mission accomplished, you cannot afford to ignore the other 80 percent, or think they are trivial to mission success. Consequently, leaders must create an environment of inspired influence that captures the souls of the uncommitted many, and transforms them into a vital part of the vision and mission success. Michael Fullan said, "When the individual soul is connected to the organization, people become connected to something deeper—the desire to contribute to a larger purpose, to feel they are part of a greater whole."[45] When everyone becomes committed to being a part of something great; then all will share the risk of failure and the probability of success.

The following passage on committment appears in W. H. Murray's *The Scottish Himalayan Expedition* (1951):

"Until one is committed, there is hesitancy, the chance to draw back, always ineffectiveness.

Concerning all acts of initiative (and creation), there is one elementary truth the ignorance of which kills countless ideas and splendid plans: that the moment one definitely commits oneself, then providence moves too. A whole stream of events issues from the decision, raising in one's favor all manner of unforeseen incidents, meetings and material assistance, which no man could have dreamt would have come his way. I learned a deep respect for one of Goethe's couplets:
Whatever you can do or dream you can, begin it. Boldness has genius, power and magic in it! "[46]

Leadership is in part about influencing; influence affects/transforms culture, culture shapes people, and people affect outcomes. So as the circle of influence increases, so do the committed few. Turning the few into the committed many is a transformation that takes place through the influence of leadership, which is the pure challenge of becoming a great leader. That transformation process may be one person at a time, but it is truly worth the effort because the most important single factor in individual success is commitment. This transformation took place in the 459th AMDS and the committed few changed into a wave of committed many who sacrificed whatever it took to get the mission accomplished.

Chapter 7 Leadership Takeaways

- "The quality of a person's life is in direct proportion to their commitment to excellence, regardless of their chosen field of endeavor."

- Leaders must create an environment of inspired influence that captures the souls of the uncommitted many, and transforms them into a vital part of the vision and mission success.

- "Whatever you can do or dream you can, begin it. Boldness has genius, power and magic in it!"

- Leadership is in part about influencing; influence affects/transforms culture, culture shapes people, and people affect outcomes. This is the essence of leadership.

- Turning the few into the committed many is a transformation that takes place through the influence of leadership, which is the pure challenge of becoming a great leader.

****

**"Life's most persistent and urgent question is:
What are you doing for others?"
~Martin Luther King, Jr.~**

****

*"Know thyself, and thy path will be revealed
Greatness is in each of us"*
Arthur R. Nicholson

Chapter 8

Being a Part of Something Great

Being a part of something great is being a part of a team with a vision, which is striving to do something great. My first experience of being a part of something great was at the early age of 11 or 12, as a member of a peewee baseball team in Clarksville, Tennessee. I played first base and outfield, on a team that had a cast of characters, as you can imagine. One person that I do remember was our pitcher. Discovering what made him successful on the pitching mound is synonymous to discovering what makes individuals successful in an organization. It was interesting that he only threw strikes consistently if he was chewing a fresh piece of bubble gum. Once we figured that out, everyone on the team brought ample amounts of bubble gum with them to each game, and so did our parents. During the game if he started getting behind on the count (balls vs. strikes), we would call time out just to make sure he had a fresh piece of gum to chew on. It was amazing how that worked.

I never really knew our coach much beyond the baseball field and practice, but ironically his name was Mr. Best and we called him Coach Best. As baseball seasons go, we won some, lost some, and at regular season end found ourselves in the playoffs. I do not remember much of the play offs, but the championship game has had a profound and lasting effect on my life. The game was classic in that it was hard fought by the two best peewee teams in Clarksville, Tennessee. My team was home team, which means that we were last at bat.

I am not sure if the game went extra endings, but of course, the score was tied at our last at bat. I was the lead off batter and somehow managed to get on first base. Next, I remember stealing second base, but it was very close. I think that I was hit to third, but it does not matter how I got there, because all that mattered was that I potentially represented the winning run.

Just as in taking command 39 years later, this was a moment of stark realization that the failure or success of the team depended on the failure or success of me getting to home plate. Thoughts of doubt did not run through my mind as they did when I took command, because at that point in the game I was running off pure adrenalin. Even at that age, I knew that this was one of those pivotal moments, given the significance of being the potential winning run that would end the game and place our team in the history books as the peewee champs.

At this point in the game, the drama was at its highest with two outs, two men on (first and third) and the winning run less than 90 feet from home plate. The umpire called "batter up," and we knew that a hit or a steal to home plate was our only options to win the game. My memory has faded, and I am not sure if we got a hit or if I stole home, but I do remember having to slide into home plate to make it, and I think I went in headfirst. No matter how I got there, I was called safe, and the celebration began.

Coach Best seemed to be at home plate before I got there, because to my surprise he had picked me up, and was holding me high in the air shouting we won, we won, over and over again. Dust was flying, I was a mess, the players were jumping up and down and the parents were going wild. My mother actually fainted during the excitement. Our team's picture was in the local newspaper as the champions of the Clarksville peewee league, underscoring that Coach Best's team was the best, and we were a part of something great.

In baseball, as in life, there is a winner and a loser. On that day, the other team experienced as great a loss as we did a win. Of course, they were not happy, some were crying, others were just silent and yet others were simply dejected from the hard fought game. What was significant is that every one of them lined up and congratulated each of us on our win. Although they were hurt from not winning the game, I think we all respected the undeniable fact that everyone left all of their individual and shared effort to win, on the field that day.

Just as in other life experiences, giving it all we had to give that day, yielded a byproduct called humility. The humility that I speak of here was born out of the effort expended by each player, and his respect for the hard fought game. The humility in effect took the individual factor away, and replaced it with team effort and spirit. It also served to take some of the sting and disappointment out of losing, as well as tempered the over the top celebration and exhilaration of winning.

As a footnote to this experience, when I have not given my all, it has surely haunted me, win or lose. I remember that day as one of the greatest moments in my life because it taught me so much about life, at an early age. Amazingly, after writing this section of the book, months later I actually found a letter written to me by Coach Best, in 1984, which I have presented on the next page. I was truly humbled to read his thoughts.

Letter from Coach Best

Herschel C. Best
Route 11, Box 546
Peterson Lane
Clarksville, Tennessee 37040
March 5, 1984

Lt. Arthur Nicholson
12070 Monte Drive
Bridgeton, Missouri 63044

Dear Arthur:

I wish it were possible to tell you how much I am pleased to learn you have completed Officer Training School and commissioned a Lieutenant in the United States Air Force. I must have overlooked the graduate list in the Air Force Times. I retired from the Air Force in 1961 as First Sergeant.

Your graduation from Officer Training School further assures me that our championship Little League team players were the very best group of young men a Coach would desire to have around. I have worked with many teams and ours is the best group, not only in ability, but, outstanding in every way.

Your parents seemed surprised and pleased that I remembered all the players after 16 years. Henry Baggett, Joe Brewer, J.D. Bumpas, Gary Cook, Rodney Davis, John Fletcher, Jim Harker, Ronnie Harrison, Bill Martin, James Merriweather, Arthur Nicholson, Richard Petty, Vince Vaughn, and Melvin Wisdom. As you remember, I gave every player the opportunity to play in every game. Our starting lineup was VAUGHN - LF, NICHOLSON - 1B, BUMPAS - 3B, FLETCHER - C, HARKER - SS, PETTY - CF, BREWER - 2B, DAVIS - RF, MERRIWEATHER - P. Do you remember the play we put on in the All Star game? You stole home with the winning run.

Arthur, you have made your old Coach very proud. I hope I am around when you are promoted to General. I sure hope you will visit me when you are home on leave. Your English teacher at Greenwood School (Mrs. Bright) is also my daughter. She sends you her very best wishes.

Your Mother told me you were stationed in Oklahoma, however, I am of the opinion you are at Scott Air Force Base, Illinois. I hope you will have time to write and I promise to answer all your letters.

Sincerely yours,

Herschel C. Best

Chapter 8 Leadership Takeaways

- Being a part of something great is being a part of a team with a vision, which is striving to do something great.

- Giving it all you have to give, yields a byproduct called humility.

- Humility in effect takes the individual factor away and replaces it with team effort and spirit.

- Make the effort to stay in touch with your mentors because their wisdom will flatten your learning curve and grow your leadership toolbox.

****

**What you get
By reaching your
destination
Is not as important
As what you become
By reaching your
destination.**

****

Dare to walk the Edge,
where there are no footprints to follow,
where there are no footprints left behind,
Dare to walk the Edge,
that the path that leads to where you are cannot be seen,
that you can only relate to its existence on a spiritual level,
that others can only realize your journey on that same level,
Dare to walk the Edge

Arthur R. Nicholson

Chapter 9

Practicing LAP

(The package)

This concept has been developed over many years of experience with individuals, organizations, and personal situations. "Practicing LAP" is a way of living and leading as an individual. Many have conceptualized, written, and taught about Leadership, Accountability, and Professionalism for centuries. What I have done is package them into the phrase "Practicing LAP" to facilitate a leadership culture that is servant based, relational, visionary, and inspiring. Individuals who embody LAP will display initiative, integrity, accountability, responsibility, and compassion on a personal and professional level.

(The action)

Practicing LAP starts on an individual level. We must develop the tenets of LAP internally to connect with the leader within in order to first lead ourselves, then to serve others in a leadership capacity. That means that we have to be sure of where we stand on integrity, what our values are, what we will live for, and ultimately, what we will die for. Our passions, our strengths, our weaknesses, our limits personally and professionally will also have to be pondered. There are times during our practice of LAP, when we may choose to stand alone, and it is those times that we surely must know on what principle or principles we are standing. Our foundations should be solid and built on the bedrock of the wisdom of self. "Know thyself well or get to know thyself well, while one is catching up with the person that one needs to be." I assure you that is a race that we do not want to find ourselves in very often as leaders.

I believe that we all have learned the definitions of LAP, and can pass the academic test. However, the actual practice of LAP on a continuum is sorely lacking on an individual level as well as in many organizations. Approximately one-third of followers reveal that they have never worked for, or been motivated by, an exceptional leader.[47] Additionally, over 60 per cent of followers report that their leaders are out of touch with how people are feeling.[48] Furthermore, most can talk it, but few walk in the footsteps of LAP and leave a visible trail for others to follow. Some walk through their leadership roles leaving an impact synonymous and indicative of the footprints left from a walk on the beach before the tide roles in. After the tide roles out, our footprints are forever washed away and no one would ever know that we were there.

I challenge you to build a lighthouse through the practice of LAP so that all that may follow will be guided, developed, and inspired to the highest levels of their individual potential as leaders in any endeavor they desire or may find themselves.

After mastering the individual aspects of practicing LAP, the next level is about fusing the tenants of leadership, accountability and professionalism into a demeanor of leadership that not only influences mission accomplishment, but also most importantly inspires individuals. At this point, your behavior will make a statement of your leadership potential without you ever uttering a word. You will be walking the talk. Practicing LAP is not a badge for show, instead, it is an existence of inspired servant leadership that has its origin as an internal stillness that flows outward.

Missions are why organizations exist. The leadership positions in those organizations come and go, but the impact of practicing LAP that is made on individuals is lasting, and leaves footprints of your inspiration that will not be washed away with the tide of time. Leaders should ensure that the practice of LAP is cultivated on individual and organizational levels so that LAP becomes a part of the organizational culture. This approach will give birth to the lasting effects of practicing LAP on all levels. This concept is meant to target the whole person and manifest its effects through the person practicing it to those around that person. That means the practice of LAP should be evident in all of the roles (airman, father, mother, supervisor, CEO) that we play in a given day, week or month.

Take a LAP

As a footnote to the concept of Practicing LAP, I shared with the members that if I asked them to "take a lap" that meant that one of the elements of LAP was notably missing in their practice of LAP. If I asked an airman to take a couple of laps, they really needed to take stock in their commitment to the vision that I had laid out. Lastly, if I asked one to take 10 or more laps, that meant that they needed to start looking for another place to be, because I was going to dedicate myself to making that happen. Of course, I made these statements as a play on the words of practicing LAP versus running a lap. Nevertheless, each member knew that I was ultra serious about the practice of LAP. I believe that the practice of LAP as a parent, teacher, church member, first line manager, CEO or Commander is the first step to becoming a great leader. You in turn, will be building great leaders to accomplish something great.

LAP and Core Values

"The core values of an organization are those values we hold which form the foundation on which we perform work and conduct ourselves. In an ever-changing world, core values are constant. Core values are not descriptions of the work we do or the strategies we employ to accomplish our mission. Core values are the basic elements of how we go about our work, define how we interact with each other and which strategies we employ to fulfill our mission."[49]

From a leadership/organizational perspective, the practice of LAP can, and should, be woven into an organization's core values. LAP shares a very fundamental connection, and is an out-growth of the Air Force Core Values that I have embraced. The Air Force Core values are "Integrity first, Service before self, and Excellence in all we do."[50] The components of LAP (leadership, accountability, professionalism) and their practice is a continuum of personification based on the solid foundation of the Air Force Core Values. Every component of LAP can be associated and supported with each of the Air Force Core Values.

The more we are able to connect the dots between practicing LAP and our personal or organizational core values, the more stability and longevity will the concept of practicing LAP be enjoyed in our lives, and our organizations.

Chapter 9 Leadership Takeaways

- Practicing LAP starts on an individual level.
- Practicing LAP facilitates a leadership culture that is servant based, relational, visionary, and inspiring.

- Practicing LAP is a way of living and leading as a leader to facilitate a culture of initiative, responsibility, and sensitivity on a personal and professional level.

- "Know thyself well or get to know thyself well while one is catching up with the person that one needs to be."

- The impact of practicing LAP that is made on individuals is lasting, and leaves footprints of your influence that are not washed away with the tide of time.

- Practicing LAP is about fusing the tenants of leadership, accountability and professionalism into a demeanor of leadership that not only influences the mission of the organization but most importantly its people.

- The components of LAP (leadership, accountability, professionalism) and their practice is a continuum of personification based on the solid foundation of Organizational Core Values.

"We become what we think. Therefore our challenge as leaders, is to foster an environment built on trust, increasing responsibility, and recognition which manifests and motivates individuals to think of themselves as an integral part of the mission, and accordingly act in a manner that achieves the ultimate objectives."

Arthur R. Nicholson

Chapter 10

Leadership

Effective leadership is one of the most important and pressing needs of the day, as leadership is one of the most critical and compelling issues facing the world. Leadership is both the essence of influencing and the art of inspiring others. To me that is simply leaving others in a better place. Specifically, it is helping others realize and develop their fullest potential as leaders in whatever endeavor they may find themselves. Reading about leadership is a great way to learn about this craft conceptually, but actually practicing leadership is what counts. It counts because our practice creates good and bad experiences/outcomes from which to learn/grow.

Whether a very youthful leader or more mature in years as I, we all take our cues largely from those who have actually led us in some capacity. We take note of those we have followed and adopt what works to our own style to produce positive results/outcomes. Be it good leadership or bad, in the end it is all about outcomes (that which our leadership influences). In one of the first conversations that I had with a member of the 459th AMDS, I was asked to be above all things, a Commander that leads.

Leadership Influence vs. Inspiration

There has been much written about leadership influence and/or inspiration on one's actions. In some literature these terms are used interchangeably, while in other writings inspiring is depicted as a higher form of leadership. I have concluded that "leaders influence actions and inspire visions." Curt Cacioppo (composer, pianist) wrote: "Inspiration is the recognition of something perhaps already present in the deepest self, and in any case only knowable intimately." By contrast, "influence is a force that may spring from any point in the surrounding cultural environment. The difference between them is that an artist can choose to respond to influence, while inspiration is felt on too deep a level for discourse."[51]

Checklist Leadership

There is leadership that seems to follow a checklist for success without emotion or passion for anything. I call this type of leadership "leadership by recipe." It is like the output of a production line, the results of this type of leadership will be the same no matter who the leader is, as long as they are competent to follow the checklist/recipe. Note that this type of leader and leadership has its place in any organization and should be valued for its consistency and predictability. Also note, that its place is in a stable organizational environment where the outcomes or results meet the customer needs. This type of leader identifies most with positional leadership, which is based on the level of influence, given the leader position, that one can exert on a situation or people. Accordingly, if leadership is in part influencing, the measure of success of an uninspired leader is directly proportional to the position of influence that the leader holds. While this type of leadership is consistent and predictable, it pales in comparison to inspired leadership in thoughts, words, or deeds.

Inspired Leadership

After creating the vision for the 459th AMDS, my challenge was to inspire others to embrace the vision. I was also in a position to influence actions toward the accomplishment of the vision. Inferred above in Mr. Cacioppo's comments, is the concept that the more inspired one is, the less influence it takes for one to initiate and sustain actions in support of a vision. This actually occurred throughout my command as we turned the committed few into the committed many with inspiring leadership.

Great leaders are inspired leaders whose leadership is influential and inspiring. Leadership under the umbrella of LAP is an inspiring endeavor, producing outcomes that are nonlinear, and results that only are produced by inspired people. This type of leadership is not cookie cutter, checklist/recipe oriented leadership. Inspired leaders lead with passion, intuition, courage, vision, integrity, and they lead by example. They ask nothing of their followers that they would not do first. If this leader asks you to walk a mile, he or she will take the first step. Inspired leadership is synonymous with change leadership. The leader that embraces LAP is a leader that embraces change. Richard Oliver says "new leaders must be inspired and inspiring."[52] "In particular, they must:
- Be able to find and hold a vision while enthusing others to share that vision.
- Manage chaos and complexity while instilling enough stability to ensure smooth daily operations.

- Be able to change direction very quickly without losing the support of their stakeholders.
- Manage creatively the emotional impact of constant change."[53]

Identify a failing organization and you have simultaneously identified a failure of leadership. Likewise, find an organization achieving excellence (profit or nonprofit) and you will find the highest levels of inspired servant leadership taking care of the mission, as well as the people. Every aspect of an organization's success or failure can be directly or indirectly traced to the effectiveness or ineffectiveness of its leadership. If you aspire to be a leader, no matter the level on which you lead, you must first accept the accountability and responsibility that comes with the position. If you do otherwise, you will fail. Some organizations and situations are easier to lead than others, but make no mistake about it, all need effective leadership.

Along with the awesome opportunity and responsibility of leading, I want to share some other aspects of leadership that I experienced as a Commander. First and foremost, I recognized that when in a leadership position, people expect you to lead. That meant taking the initiative to make things happen. It is not enough to identify what needs to be done; you have to lead the charge to get it done. In short, you must lead by example.

The Loneliness of Leadership

Being out front, leading the charge is inherently a lonely place. In his book A *Failure of Nerve: Leadership in the Age of the Quick Fix,* Dr. Edwin Friedman said, "One of the major limitations of imagination's fruits is the fear of standing out. It is more than the fear of criticism. It is anxiety at being alone, of being in a position where one can rely little on others, a position that puts one's resources to the test, a position where one will have to take total responsibility for one's own response. Leaders must not only *not* be afraid of that position; they must come to love it."[54] The loneliness that I speak of has nothing to do with exclusivity of the position you hold as a leader. It is the complexity of leading, inspiring, nurturing, and sometimes disciplining those you lead, all the while keeping your eyes on the mission to be accomplished.[55]

In fact, if you are perceived as unapproachable, insensitive, and aloof, you will not be given the opportunity to engage on a personal level with individuals of your organization. That is the first step in the direction of failing your people and the mission. The loneliness is related to the sheer responsibility of being a true servant leader, knowing that the failure or success of the organization is largely and directly related to how you perform as a leader. Along with being tested and lonely at times, my experience was challenging, humbling, inspiring, frustrating and above all a much appreciated journey.

Leading with Passion

Leading with intense passion is the number one difference in peak performers and the rest of the pack.[56] Norman Vincent Peale said, "Your enthusiasm will be infectious, stimulating and attractive to others. They will love you for it. They will go for you, and with you."[57] In the military, as in other organizations, checking the box for having served in certain positions (Commander) is in some cases a prerequisite for the opportunity to serve at higher levels of responsibility. Some do just that; check the box. With the benefit of hind site, I know that given the challenges that I faced as a Commander, (as do others in similar leadership roles) without intense passion for the job, I would have surely failed. "Passion is what happens when who you are connects with what you do. It is what will get you through the hard times."[58]

I relate my experience without passion to that of a long distance runner unprepared and unenthused about the race he is about to undertake. He or she will experience excruciating pain, dissatisfaction, and frustration during the race, but these things will not knock one out of the race. It is the lack of passion that will rob one of the vision of the finish line and lead to failure. Tom Peters said, "Passionate leaders have the energy and drive needed to push and pull their teams and organizations forward. This rousing passion is the energy source that powers the technology, systems, and processes that boost personal, team, and organizational performance to ever higher levels."[59] If you possess the passion for the level of leadership necessary to meet the challenges of peak performers, let that passion live, and lead now.

Leading with Integrity

The following example of leadership in action, brings together the above thoughts on leadership as practiced under the umbrella of "Practicing LAP." Thirteen members of my unit (932 Aeromedical Staging Squadron, Scott AFB IL) deployed to Kirkuk, Iraq in June, 2003. We joined up with others from various units to form a Contingency Aeromedical Staging Facility (CASF) with the mission of staging injured warriors for air evacuation to higher levels of care. Kirkuk was a strategic military location, and we expected many casualties during our tour, which did materialize.

During the last two weeks of the tour, I was awakened in the middle of the night by a frantic knock at my tent door. After realizing that my awakening was not another call to take cover because of possible incoming rockets, I scrambled to get dressed and answered the door. At the door was a visibly shaken airman who had just gotten notification that her grandfather was gravely ill and was only given days to live. This young airman happened to be a part of the thirteen members from Scott AFB, IL. After briefly listening to her story through her tears, I quickly got the rest of my gear, and we headed for the medical control center to get more information about the situation, and alert our Commander.

We learned from the Red Cross that the airman's grandfather was not considered a part of the immediate family, thus did not come under the rules for emergency leave from the Area Of Operations (AOR). This information added insult to injury because this airman's grandparents raised her, and she considered them her legitimate parents in every way. This is where things really got dicey. We contacted our Commander, and apprised him of all of the information and requested his assistance in moving the mountain to get this airman home as soon as possible. Given that we could not send her home via the emergency leave system, we had to request permission from our headquarters for her early (2 weeks) release. This request carried with it considerations for reduced overall manpower, specialty reduction, casualty expectations, replacement manpower, and a host of other issues related to mission capability.

Further complicating this request was the fact that we had already released another individual improperly from the AOR without replacement, and without higher headquarters' approval two weeks earlier. We were still answering the mail on that issue, while facing the current dilemma. Needless to say, there was hesitancy from unit leadership to make the request, based on our previous mistakes and further shortage of manpower. This was truly a situation of A

Dancing On The Razor's EDGE

Dance On The Razor's EDGE with respect to deciding what to stand for, making the tough call, standing alone, taking care of the mission/people, and executing from the gut, based on the right thing to do.

Without going through the intense, heated, and at some points very volatile conversations with leadership about what was the right thing to do, given all due considerations, we ultimately made the request to higher headquarters for her early release. After convincing headquarters that we were sufficiently manned for any contingencies, approval was granted. The hard part of it all was not making the request, getting the approval, or getting the airman transportation back home; it was the internal organizational struggle of dealing with mistakes of the past, and the paralysis of initiative, based on fear, to take action.

The first time I saw the airman, after returning to home station, was an experience that I will never forget; and it brings chills to me as I relate this story. She literally lunged at me with tears streaming down her face, thanking me profusely for my efforts in getting her released to go home. She had gotten home just in time to spend three days with her grandfather before he died. Her grandmother told her that she knew her grandfather was waiting on her to return before he gave into his illness. Six years later, she still thanks me when she sees me. I was truly touched by this experience, and her gratitude validated that we made the right decision.

There was a leadership integrity lesson learned by all who were involved in that situation. Lead with integrity because when you have to make a stand, even if you have to stand alone, you will be standing on solid ground. Defending your position from a solid foundation makes a difference. Those who took a gut check on the above situation, made a leadership decision from within, and made the difference in one person's life. That is what leading under the umbrella of "Practicing LAP" is all about.

Taking Care of Yourself

This is a great place to talk about taking care of yourself as a leader. That means taking care of the physical, mental, and spiritual part of you so that you can stay out front of the pack to lead. If you are a servant leader, you will be focused on taking care of everyone else's needs, and it is easy to neglect your own needs. As stated before, leadership can be a lonely and exhausting place so you have to take time to collect, reflect, and project. Leaders should collect from past experiences to gain wisdom; reflect on the present to gain perspective; and project on the future to gain advantage.

To sustain a position of leadership that is inspiring, one must first find the balance within that is itself, self-inspiring. Just like flying jets, you must figure out how to keep your energy level high to be there for others when their energy level is low and the going gets tough. I developed, and use the "collect, reflect, project" approach because that is what works for me, but everyone is different, and you must figure out what works for you, and stick to that program.

Chapter 10 Leadership Takeaways

- Leadership is both the essence of influencing and the art of inspiring others.

- A vision without action is dead.

- The difference between influence and inspiration is that one can choose to respond to influence, while inspiration is felt on too deep a level for discourse."

- If leadership is in part influencing, the measure of success of an uninspired leader is directly proportional to the position of influence that the leader holds.

- Leadership under the umbrella of LAP is an inspiring endeavor, producing outcomes that are nonlinear, and outcomes that only are produced by being inspired.

- Inspired leadership is synonymous with change leadership.

- Identify a failing organization and you have simultaneously identified a failure of leadership.

- The loneliness of leadership has nothing to do with exclusivity of the position you hold as a leader, as much as it is the complexity of leading, inspiring, nurturing, and sometimes disciplining those you lead.

- Leading with intense passion is the number one difference in peak performers and the rest of the pack.

- Lead with integrity because when you have to make a stand, even if you have to stand alone, you will be standing on solid ground.

- Leadership can be a lonely and exhausting place, so take time out to collect, reflect, and project.

****

"If you give more than you ask you will almost always receive more than you expect."
~ARN~

****

*"I have never regretted my failures,
not one of them, but I have always
regretted not having given my all
to succeed, when I have fallen."*
                                                Arthur R. Nicholson

Chapter 11

Accountability

While accountability may not be as intriguing a subject to discuss as leadership, it is critical to individual and organizational success. Practicing LAP without accountability is like driving blindfolded with earplugs inserted. If we cannot see where we are going, or at least hear instructions of where to turn, then how can we be held accountable for where we end up. Therefore, leaders must have a clear vision from which to lead, be receptive to feedback, and be capable of communicating precisely to others about the direction we are leading. Leaders on any level must first understand what is being asked of them before making the commitment to performance at that level. If we then commit, accountability is in part about doing the best that we can to meet stated objectives.

Leadership Accountability

Accountability in the practice of LAP on any level is first about self-governance. In short that means doing what you committed to do. Accountability of our actions as leaders has a definite impact on our followers. Our accountability is the acknowledgment and assumption of responsibility for actions, decisions, and policies including the administration, governance and implementation within the scope of our position. This acknowledgment encompasses the obligation to report, explain and be accountable for resulting consequences.[60]

One of the members of the 459th AMDS said great leaders always lead by example. In doing so, leaders consistently demonstrate personal accountability, which sows the seed of accountability in those we lead, and ultimately creates a climate for developing organizational accountability. Leadership accountability is like swimming in a fish bowl. That means all eyes are on us from every direction, and we cannot afford to diminish the important of being congruent in our speech and our actions. All who aspire to be leaders must be prepared to accept the accountability that goes with leading. You cannot have one without the other, because just as leadership and followership are two sides of the same coin, so is leadership and accountability.

Creating a culture of Accountability

Leaders cannot be in all places at all times to monitor the activities of those we lead. Consequently, it is imperative that we create a culture of accountability within our organizations if we are to achieve the success of our vision. Developing and maintaining a culture of organizational accountability encompasses a combined culture of individual accountability, which is a continious process. Leaders must create a process that supports individual and organizational situational awareness through the lens of individual accountability. Situational awareness is: *"An informational perspective and skill that fosters an ability to determine quickly the context and relevance of events that are unfolding."*[61]

Accountability as defined above, when viewed on an individual level, is about acknowledging ownership for outcomes/results. The lens of individual accountability created in the 459th AMDS served as a vector for individuals to perform and execute with a keen sense of situational awareness. The interconnectivity of individuals practicing accountability creates organizational situation awareness. This process yields the ability to clearly visualize events and effects as they are about to unfold, enabling leaders to accelerate and synchronize decision processes, in a more responsive, proactive manner.[62]

The individual accountability process that we established is as follows:

- Establish expectations and clearly communicate them.
- Establish consequences for compliance and non-compliance and clearly communicate them.
- Establish measurement criteria for success and clearly communicate them.
- Support training that refines skills to meet expectations.
- Measure results.
- Take corrective action and follow through.
- Leaders must be approachable.
- Leaders must be flexible and consistant.
- Leaders must be the continious drum beat of accountability.
- Leaders must value individual and collective effort.
- Leaders must admonish in private and praise in public.

The Absence of Accountability

When I arrived at the 459th AMDS, there was a backlog of 58 plus performance reports. Performance Reports are required for Officers once a year, and every two years for enlisted personnel. Howerver, some Officers had up to four performance reports outstanding. Performance reports are critical to an airman's career with regard to assignments, promotions, and ultimately one's existence in the organization. Along with a multitude of other issues, this situation pointed directly to a lack of accountability that needed to be addressed immediately. We did address these issues through the individual accountability process described above. Appproximately one year after we implemented the process, there were no performance reports overdue. That result took the united effort of individuals who acknowledged ownership of the process and executed in a manner commensurate with leadership expectations.

No matter the venue, family, private organizations, or government, one of the reasons for failure is the inability of establishing accountability through effective leadership. People will lower their performance to the lowest possible level acceptable to the leader, simply because they do not feel that they will be held accountable for their behavior. In contrast, when leaders set the standard of accountability by their own behavior, and communicate their expectations to the organization with very clear consequences for compliance or noncompliance, a culture for individual and organizational accountability is established. Accountability is the cornerstone of empowering people to act with initiative, excel in performance, and accept responsibility for their actions.

A Leadership Imperative

Individual and organizational accountability is a leadership imperative. The practice of LAP without accountability is like trying to sit on a three-legged stool with one leg missing. It is pretty hard to do. Leaders must understand that accountability is not something that is simply enforced; more accurately, it is accepted. Accordingly, there should be established consequences for lack of accountability. These consequences have to be consistently applied. There is a saying that what does not get measured does not get done.

Likewise, we should praise and celebrate, openly, individual and organizational accountability because our actions reinforce and energize the maintenance of accountability. The creation and maintenance of individual and organizational accountability is a high-energy, continuous leadership endeavor. The key is setting the example, which supports an accountability culture that establishes an automatic self-policing process throughout the organization.

Chapter 11 Leadership Takeaways

- All leaders on any level must first understand what is being asked of them before we make the commitment to performance at that level.

- Accountability in the practice of LAP on any level is first about self-governance.

- Accountability of one's actions as a leader resonates with one's followers; it is about performance and owning up to the outcome of that to which one has committed.

- Accountability is the cornerstone of empowering people to act with initiative, excel in performance, and accept responsibility for their actions.

- The bottom line is that a leader's behavior is either consistent or inconsistent with what he or she is saying.

- All who aspire to be leaders must be prepared to accept the accountability that goes with leading.

- The key is setting the example which supports an accountability culture that establishes an automatic self-policing process throughout the organization.

****

**"If you talk more
than you do,
You will get done less than
what you say.
But if you think more
than you talk,
And talk less than you do
All of what you talk and
most of what you think
Will be done."
~ARN~**

****

Watch your thoughts, for they become words.
Watch your words, for they become actions.
Watch your actions, for they become habits.
Watch your habits, for they become character.
Watch your character, for it becomes your destiny.
                                    Author Unknown

Chapter 12

Professionalism

A leader's professionalism under the umbrella of practicing LAP is not only about where one is leading others, or even one's ability to lead; it is about how one leads others that matters. The "how" packages the "where" and the "ability." There is a saying that leading without followers is just taking a walk in the park. When leaders do not fuse their vision and ability to lead, with relationship building fostered through professionalism, we are just taking a walk in the park.

To introduce the concept of leadership professionalism under LAP, I would like to propose two questions. In a life or death immediate situation, do we care how much professionalism the person saving us displays? My answer would be a resounding, NO! However, if we were afflicted with a chronic or terminal illness, where we have to receive care over an extended period, would we care how much professionalism the person caring for us displays? My answer would be, YES, based on all of the aspects of professionalism that come into play with time spent, personal interaction, and the psychological aspects of healing that are all components of a relationship with the caretaker.

One may be of the opinion that as long as their life is being prolonged, and/or they are being kept comfortable, it does not matter who is treating them. While I agree in this case that the illness is being properly managed clinically, the influence of the psychological aspects of healing through a positive relationship with the provider cannot be categorically dismissed. The trust of the relationship that must be established between a patient and provider to foster continued interaction toward healing is the same trust relationship that a leader must nurture in followers to influence and inspire action toward a vision. Both relationships are about how one interacts to deliver or perform, as professionals, the skills of their profession.

Professionalism Defined

The American College Dictionary defines profession, professional, and professionalism as follows:[63]

A **profession** is "a vocation *requiring* knowledge of some department of learning or science."

A **professional** is one who follows "an occupation as a means of livelihood or gain," or one who is "engaged in one of the *learned* professions."

Professionalism is exhibited by one of the "*professional character, spirit or methods*" or the "standing, practice, or methods of a professional as *distinguished from an amateur*."

Dr. Stuart Kinsinger defines Professionalism as service through the use of specialized knowledge, skills, and experience; holding oneself to the highest standards of thought, word, and deed.[64] The term "professional character," in particular, denotes moral qualities, ethical standards, and principles which are elements present in both definitions. In my study of leadership, I have defined professionalism in my own terms as, "the manner in which one carries out or performs their profession." This definition is further expanded by stating that professionalism is the lasting effect of the manner in which one performs his or her profession.

The Face of Professionalism

Unfortunately, not all professionals practice professionalism. I have experienced instances of leadership where professionalism made a profound difference in the lasting effect of whatever the service rendered. Accordingly, professionalism is NOT about how many degrees and certificates one has attained, or to how many professional associations one belongs. Professionalism is the character wrapped around and through that which we, as professionals, so skillfully do. The practice of professionalism under the umbrella of LAP is fundamentally relational in nature. The following are some attributes of professionalism:[65]

Collaboration: Working with others to achieve a common goal.

Honesty and Integrity: Demonstrating truthfulness, professional behavior, and trustworthiness.

Respect: Honors, values, and demonstrates consideration and regard for oneself and others.

Commitment to Continuous Learning: Values learning for self and profession.

Emotional Maturity: Demonstrates situational awareness and appropriate behavior.

Leadership and Responsibility: Acts independently and demonstrates accountability, reliability, and sound judgment.

I add to this list, Service before self, Integrity, and Excellence in all we do, which are the Air Force Core Values. As leaders, we must conduct ourselves professionally and promote the practice of professionalism in our organizations.

Professionalism is not a behavior practiced only in interaction with the customer; it should be evident in our relationships with subordinates, peers, and superiors. The manner in which we lead defines the face (character) of our leadership and the lasting effects of our leading shape the legacy of our leadership. The character and the legacy of our leadership are directly related to the professionalism that we practice as leaders.

Chapter 12 Leadership Takeaways

- LAP is not only about where one is leading others or even one's ability to do so; it is about how one leads others that matters.

- When leaders do not fuse their vision and ability to lead with relationship building fostered through professionalism, we are just taking a walk in the park.

- Professionalism is the character wrapped around and through that which we as professionals so skillfully do.

- Professionalism is the manner in which we lead, which defines the face (character) of our leadership and the lasting effects of our leading that shape the legacy of our leadership.

- The face (character) and the lasting effect of our leadership are directly related to the professionalism that we practice as leaders.

****

**"It is hardest to help
one understand
what he knows not,
especially when the one
who knows not,
knows he knows."
~ARN~**

****

"Each of us must dig down inside to find ourselves;
you will only have to dig in proportion to the depth
to which you have buried the true you."
                    Arthur R. Nicholson (Jan 1992)

Chapter 13

Turning the Corner

(*Being patient*)

Turning the corner, seeing the light at the end of the tunnel, or finally seeing the evidence of what you have believed in, takes time, patience, and faith in your vision. When I thought about how to relate how hard it is to keep the faith in your vision, I thought about a saying that I always heard growing up, which was: "the patience of Job." I researched its origin and found that the expression is a characterization of a man named Job in the Bible. My intent in relating the story of Job here, is not to compare my story with the ordeal of Job, but to share the wisdom of holding on to your vision through faith and patience.

The Story of Job

The story of Job in the Bible refers to Job's refusal to condemn God in the face of many setbacks, and the test of his faith in life. Job was very prosperous and had seven sons and three daughters. Satan killed all Job's animals, destroyed his farm, killed all his children, and eventually gave Job boils. Using all his patience and faith, Job lasted through all of this, never questioning or condemning God. As the story goes, Job was restored to health, gaining double the riches he possessed before, and having seven sons and three daughters. His new daughters were the most beautiful in the land, and were given inheritance along with their brothers. Job was blessed once again, and lived another 140 years after the ordeal, living to see his children to the fourth generation, and dying peacefully of old age.[66] Those of you who are already Commanders or leaders of organizations, can surely relate to "the patience of Job" which must be practiced as you lead your respective organizations.

War Time Readiness

At the 459th AMDS, our symbol or mark for turning the corner was a statistic called Individual Medical Readiness (IMR). This statistic was a measure of the medical readiness of an individual to go to war or to be deployed on an operational mission. The acceptable rate for the Air Force Reserves at the time I was in command was 70 percent, which meant that at any given time, a unit had to show that 70 percent of its members were medically fit to fight. This statistic was viewed at the highest levels of the command, and became a single point (report card) for measuring the health and readiness of an organization.

When I took command, the wing was at 34 percent compliance. If there ever was a rallying point, this was one, and I immediately recognized it as such. Successfully raising this statistic was the underpinning of success in a lot of other areas in the unit and the wing. To do so, took the integrated effort of every member in the wing, from an accountability point of view.

At the unit level we had to not only create consistent processes for affecting a positive outcome, we had to also meticulously document each member's medical record with the evidence that proved compliance. There is a saying that what is not measured does not get done, and at this point we did not have a set of metrics that consistently measured what was getting done or that projected what needed to be done.

My goal was to design a set of metrics, that at a glance, would tell me where we were with respect to the IMR statistical goal, and to measure the overall operational capability of the unit. We had to focus on both, because to be medically ready without the operational capability was a no go.

Creating IMR Stat Accountability

To make sure the vital IMR statistic got the visibility that it needed in the wing, I presented all of the IMR statistics monthly, by both unit and group, to the Wing Commander (or CEO in civilian terms). This accomplished three very important things: it helped to keep the focus and support of the Wing Commander, it created a sense of accountability among the Commanders for their respective units and group statistics, and it also served as a competitive tool among the Commanders, as no one wanted their unit to show a lack of progression each month. These actions served as a way of sparking healthy competition in which everyone could be a winner when the goal was achieved, because every unit had to progress for the good of the whole.

Creating Continuous Support for the Vision

There were twenty units and four groups in the wing, which accounted for approximately 1,300 members. Each unit had a different operational mission, which carried with it a unique set of challenges to overcome to ensure compliance with the IMR mandate. The 459th AMDS was the focal point for mitigating each of these challenges, with respect to ensuring each unit had the accessibility to all of the medical services that was necessary to address each component of the IMR readiness statistic. Medically speaking, this was a laborious process, to say the least, and at times, it took every ounce of practicing LAP to get it done. This is, for sure, where patience and faith in your vision has to be revisited and communicated to the masses every chance you get.

A leader has to be creative about presenting the vision in different ways and on different levels, so that everyone has a chance to understand their part of the mission. This continuous crystallization of the vision helps members in making the commitment to support the vision against all odds. If there is an art to leadership, I am of the belief that it is the capacity to communicate on all levels genuinely, and with compassion that inspires and motivates one to growth beyond themselves, for the greater good of the whole.

We measured success in small doses, sometimes one percent at a time; and we celebrated these small accomplishments at each occurrence. It is important to recognize the little successes, and put them in perspective to the overall goal. Small successes, and the celebration of them, help to keep the focus on the vision, and the end game or state. Of course, there were setbacks and disappointments along the way. At times none of our efforts seemed to stick, or if there was success in one direction, there was equal or greater failure in another direction.

The frustration level on all of us ran high, and took its toll on us, but we stayed determined to reach the goal. I remember Colonel Cohen, our Chief Flight Surgeon, relating our plight to an analogy of turning a sailboat versus an ocean liner. We were turning an ocean liner, and it took a good measure of "the patience of Job" to stay the course, and a healthy dose of faith to see things not as they were, but as they were going to be. I more related to the Cessna vs. the C-5 cargo aircraft analogy.[67] It takes a lot more thrust to get the C-5 in the air than the Cessna. Nevertheless, we all shared the frustration, but being out front as a leader is exponentially frustrating, humbling, and very lonely at times. If you are aspiring to be a leader, know that you will be tested in this manner. Consequently, your ability to endure, and overcome this test, will be the measure of your wisdom, humility, and greatness as a leader. That may sound good, and it is true, but in the thick of it all, (the fog of war) you, as I, will be just trying to figure out the way forward.

Lesson Learned

Fortunately, we did figure it out little by little, month after month, and we made progressive movements toward our goal. One of my lessons learned was to determine when and where to apply pressure as well as when not to apply it. At one point during my quest to prove a point, I asked our members what was the worst type of bleeding that they as a medical member would encounter, and told them to be clear on what decisive actions to take. Some said "arterial," others said "head injury," but none got it right.

I told them that internal bleeding, in my mind, was the worst kind for several reasons. First, you cannot see it, or know its level of diffusion. Secondly, if you cannot see it you cannot apply the correct amount of pressure or the right procedure to stop it. The lesson that I learned, and that I related to them, is that to make consistent measurable progress toward our goals we must identify the area of need first, and judiciously apply the correct pressure (leadership) that corrects the course in a sustainable and lasting manner.

There were times when our statistics would spike positively, then plummet negatively just as fast. In most instances, we were reacting to a symptom of the problem, and not the problem itself. This will happen to the best of leaders, and the remedy was to slow down, and reevaluate the situation. As a parent, I tell my children when your world around you is going too fast, stop, and figure out which way the wind is blowing, and if at all possible walk with the wind at you back. What we did at the unit was to analyze the data from every conceivable angle to see which way the wind was truly blowing. Slowly we became better at projecting outcomes based on directed efforts. Most of these efforts were self-directed.

Leadership is about empowering those around you to make things happen, and to not immobilize individuals in place until you give the directive to go. In every instance where I was successful in creating an environment rich with empowerment for growth, individuals found the leader within, and took the initiative to find the solutions to the obstacles that we were facing. My experience has proven that to empower others is a deliberate act of relinquishing some of the power vested in me as a leader, or by virtue of my position, for the growth, and development of others. This state or level of leadership can only be achieved and exercised when one is confident with one's capacity to lead, and simultaneously willing to invest in others, for the benefit of growing them to the highest levels of their potential as leaders.

The Corner Turned

In January of 2007, our statistics were at 34 percent for the wing, and by November 2007 the wing spiked to 71 percent. I cannot truly relate how reaching 71 percent boosted the morale in the whole wing. We celebrated and high-fived for a week or more until the next update, which had dropped to 65 percent, and it was back to the grind. Reaching 71 percent was to say we could reach our goal, and now it was about sustaining it. By this time, all of the commanders were on board and understood which buttons to push to make things happen. In fact, educating the commanders and the wing members on the IMR process, and apprising them of their vested interest, was one of the most effective actions that our medical unit accomplished. Practicing LAP was a huge factor in addressing, educating, and creating a collaborative approach among wing members and commanders, wherein their own practice of LAP sealed the deal on a win-win proposition.

My experience was in no way on the level of Job's. However, I do understand, as some of you can, that sometimes leadership takes the "patience of Job." Additionally, it takes every ounce of your faith in your vision to remain on the tip of the spear, communicate, and lead an organization to successful mission accomplishment.

Chapter 13 Leadership Takeaways

- The faith and the "patience of Job" are essential and worthwhile virtues to possess as a leader.

- Find the organization's rallying point, and use it as the underpinning of success drawing on the collective effort of every member in the organization.

- If there is an art to leadership, it is the capacity to communicate on all levels with genuinness and compassion that inspires and motivates one to growth beyond themselves for the greater good of the whole.

- Know that you will be tested; to endure and overcome will be the measure of your wisdom, humility, and greatness as a leader.

- When your world around you is going too fast, stop and figure which way the wind is blowing, and if at all possible walk with the wind at you back.

- Leadership takes the "patience of Job." Additionally, it takes every ounce of your faith in your vision to remain on the tip of the spear, communicate, and lead an organization to successful mission accomplishment.

****

"True wisdom is to know the moment to apply that which you have learned and grown through, called life's lessons."
~ARN~

****

There is faith and there is action,
Action begets increased renewed faith,
therein is created a cycle by which we
stand strong in the word, and strong in our word.
                                    Arthur R. Nicholson (Aug 1993)

Chapter 14

Holding it All Together

(Keeping eyes on target)

With less than seven months until inspection (December 2007), holding it all together was like the seventh ending stretch of the baseball game where you catch your breath, and try to hold on to the lead at all cost. Holding it together in a game is not about who is on top at a given moment, but who has the momentum when it really counts. What was interesting about our organization, that was different from other medical units, is that most units trained to go to war. In contrast, we were at war every time we showed up, executing the mission of ensuring that airmen were medically ready to fight. Okay, we were not experiencing bombs and rockets, but we were put to the test each weekend that we showed up for duty. This is not unlike leaders of other organizations that have to show profit or efficiencies every time they show up. The leaders of these organizations are surely on the hook to deliver positive results and keep their eyes focused on the target.

Your eyes become theirs

When you, as a leader, are pushing your people to the limit consistently, it is hard for them to keep their eyes on the target. That becomes your job and your focus as a leader, because you are out front leading and running interference for the group. Your eyes become their eyes as you must consistently communicate, and literally transfer the vision to them when things get so thick that they cannot see beyond the next task or the immediate goal. At this point in our journey, we knew we could get to 70 percent IMR, but the real test was could we sustain that level, especially when it counted? If that statistic was the only thing to be concerned about, we were good to go, but as you can imagine, we had a host of other objectives to satisfy simultaneously.

As with any organization, there were personnel issues, process issues, oversight issues, challenges, and many other concerns that were simply out of our direct control. Dealing with all of these issues collectively is what running and leading any organization is about. It is easy to get distracted with the urgent, and not deal with the important tasks that sustain your ultimate goals. As a leader, keeping your eyes on the target is an important part of your responsibility. It is not easy, but it must be done for the successful accomplishment of the mission at hand.

Seeing the potential in others

Leaders must recognize that the task of leading cannot be accomplished alone, and must be shared. We must see the potential in others, and cultivate it to support the goals of the organization. I knew that we, as a group, needed to harvest the maximum potential in each other if we were to reach our organizational goals. There is a quote that I ran across that expresses seeing this potential in others very eloquently.

If you treat an individual as he is, he will stay as he is,
but if you treat him as if he were what he ought to be, and could be, he will become what he ought and could be.
JOHANN WOLFGANG VON
GOETHE (1749-1832)

This quote hangs on my wall to remind others, and myself, that as individuals, and especially as leaders, we must strive to see each other beyond our mistakes and our past. All too often in organizations, we cast in stone an individual's potential contributions based solely on one mistake, or one embarrassing moment. If my mentors had falsely characterized my potential based solely on some of my bone-headed decisions, I would not have been given the opportunities to prove myself beyond those shortcomings. Leaders know that mistakes will happen, and it is the spirit in which those mistakes are made that must be taken into account when assessing individual potential.

Correctly assessing individual potential is a responsibility that we as leaders must embrace, to be affective at mentoring potential leaders in our organizations. Beyond the undercurrent of mislabeled characterizations that sometimes stick for a lifetime, robbing individuals of genuine opportunities to prove themselves, is a diamond in the rough, and a genuine servant leader. We must always assess correctly one's potential to be a true asset to the organization.

I faced this dilemma many times when deciding to endorse promotions or place people in positions of authority, especially if that individual was going to have supervisory responsibilities. This is why it is so crucial to know your people from inside out; to know their strengths, their weaknesses, and to know them beyond their rank or job titles. This familiarization will allow you to place them in situations that enhance the growth of leadership from within. This approach will set the individual up for leadership success, thus promoting the ultimate success of the mission, and the organization.

I used this concept, "seeing the potential in others," as the theme in a speech (January 2008) to the unit, where I asked for 100 percent commitment toward our goals. I told the unit that the stress level was going to increase for each of us based on our efforts to exceed the 71 percent IMR statistic, ensuring that our programs were completely compliant, and holding each other absolutely accountable, as we marched toward the inspection. Although not as a Commander, I had experienced HSI preparations before, and I knew that we were in the quiet before the storm period.

A leader's challenge is to influence the preparation of his or her people on two levels; physically and mentally. All too often, it is not the physical aspect that robs us of success; it is the lack of mental preparation to persevere through the difficult times of our endeavor.

From Me to We

Holding it all together required making the correct assessment and more. It was about taking the focus off the "me" and directing it on the "we." We experienced what all organizations go through when trying to be the best. Some parts of the organization were better performers than others. This can possibly pose an unhealthy atmosphere among the departments of an organization, where the collaborative approach and the all eyes on the target mentality can break down.

At this point in the process, we were losing momentum because although everyone had responded to the call for 100 percent commitment, more energy was focused on individual effort, and programs, than contributions to the total effort. Uncertainty was a very strong contributor to stress levels that were at the highest point. There was still much to be done to pass the inspection, which solidified in our minds that this was not a done deal. Leaders should sense this negative energy, and make sure to communicate that if there is a win, we all win; and if we lose, we all lose. To bring this point out, I, in one of my rare moments, had an epiphany that I shared with the entire unit.

Before our organizational meeting in February, 2008, I was in the men's room, of all places, when this thought came to me, and I reduced my thoughts to two pieces of tissue paper. I was trying to come up with how to relate that it was not about "the me," but all about "the we" in our quest to stay on target. On one sheet of tissue, I wrote the word me, and on the other tissue I wrote the word we. The epiphany was that if you flip the ME down side up, the ME became WE. I quickly had this designed on a larger piece of paper for the demonstration to the group.

To set the presentation up, I spoke to the group emphasizing that focusing on individual or departmental goals was a good initial approach to fixing our problems. However, that approach alone would not get us to our goal of being a part of something great. I expressed that this type of energy was not about practicing LAP, and it would not serve the whole of the unit. I also expressed that each of us had a responsibility to find the leader within, and turn the focus of our individual energy from the "me" into the collective "we." At that moment, I flipped the "me" that was showing on the bottom half of the flip chart, up-side down to present the "we." Instantaneously they got it, and the rest of that day, and for some time forward, the saying around the unit was "me to we."

It was amazing how that one demonstration shifted the thought process and galvanized the unit into a collaborative approach, with all eyes focused on the common target and not on just individual or departmental accomplishments.

This was undoubtedly a pivotal moment for the organization as we were at a very critical point in turning the organization around.

My quest to demonstrate the affect of transforming from the "me" to "we' in this book is a story in itself. Fortunately, after several brain storming sessions with Ms. Linda Holton of Faith Baptist Church Publishing & Printing, the idea of a book marker surfaced as a viable option. After some intense design work, the "ME"-to-"WE" book marker was born. At the bottom of the marker, by flipping the "ME" up, the "WE" is revealed as a constant reminder to each of us that it is not about the "ME", but all about the "WE" in the team effort to make it happen.

Leaders, when you are out front leading the way and running interference, be careful to look back over your shoulder and make sure that you are being followed. It is very easy to be so focused on the target that you forget the most important part of getting there. That part is taking care of the needs of your people, which in turn takes care of the needs of the mission. So many times the leader gets to the battlefront only to discover that he is the only one poised to fight the enemy.

Great leaders stand on the shoulders of those they lead, instead of on their backs. There is, literally, a different view from that vantage point. All too often, we, as leaders, grind our people into the ground and end up standing on their backs. As an alternative, we need to look back, take care of their needs so that they can stand tall in the fight, and we in turn have the advantage of the view from their shoulders instead of their backs. If you do not believe this point of view, just lie on the floor and take a look, then stand up in a chair and compare the view. The view is much different from the vantage point of the chair, and we must have the advantage of an elevated view from which to guide our people toward the organizational goals.

Single Minded Thinking

At this point in the fight, and on our journey from broken to one of the best, it was critical to get to the point of thinking, believing, talking, and doing, single-mindedly. It was now March, 2008. We had achieved 71 percent IMR, everyone was giving 100 percent, and the focus had switched from "me" to "we." While all of that was great, we needed single-minded thinking so that we, as a group, could be seen from afar performing in formation. To be honest, as a leader, you represent the drumbeat and tempo, which encompasses thinking, believing, talking, and doing that which keeps the organization marching in unison. If you are off beat, so is the organization and just like a band marching in a parade, everyone will see it.

One example where single-mindedness is critical to mission success is formation flying. Learning to fly in a formation is very taxing physically and mentally on the leader, (lead aircraft) as well as the wingman (trailing aircraft). In the beginning neither pilot knows the other's strengths, or challenges, therefore they cannot anticipate each other. After some very concentrated training, and near death experiences, each transforms into one mind in the air, and the beauty and precision of formation flying is realized, and witnessed.

The need to develop single-minded thinking as an organization was the topic of my briefing to the unit in March, 2008, three months prior to the inspection. We also developed a document entitled *"Col. Nick's Extended LAP List For the HSI Inspection, CC's Top 10 List for Inspection Preparation."* We actually modified this list from our active duty sister organization that was also preparing for a HSI inspection. The list is as follows:

1. BRAG ABOUT YOUR PEOPLE!
2. No EXCUSES!
3. Show your loyalty.
4. Be professional!
5. Take responsibility.
6. Be honest!
7. Know the big picture.
8. Don't be taken by surprise!
9. Be positive!
10. Make a good impression!

I have realized the beauty and precision of the concerted efforts of individuals (in the air and in organizations) that have transformed into one mind to reach higher than they ever thought they could go. Those were unforgettable moments, and truly represented all eyes-on-target efforts.

Communication

In business it is all about location, location, location, and in leadership it is all about COMMUNICATION, COMMUNICATION, COMMUNICATION! Most of the setbacks or mission failures that I have experienced as a leader have not been because of lack of effort, but for lack of communication. Communication from leaders should be both affective and effective; affective enough to make an impression on the mind or motivate the feelings. It should also be effective enough to cause action and movement toward a desired state or result. If a leader is to influence, then there has to be the exact type of communication that fits the situation. If the situation is urgent, then the communication must be an order so that there is not a second thought before action takes place.

In our situation, the communication needed to be supporting, motivating, directional, inspirational, and many other adjectives to fit the ever-changing operational environment in which we found ourselves. Making sure all eyes were on target during this critical period, when we had to keep it all together, was supported by practicing LAP through affective and effective communication.

Chapter 14 Leadership Takeaways

- Your eyes become their eyes in the fog of war. As a leader, keeping eyes on target is a critical part of your responsibility.

- If you treat an individual as he is; he will stay as he is, but if you treat him as if he were what he ought to be and could be, he will become what he ought and could be.

- Each of us has a responsibility to find the leader within and turn the focus of our individual energy from the "me" into the collective "we."

- When great leaders stand on the shoulders of those they lead, instead of on their backs, there is literally a different view from that vantage point.

- Leaders represent the drumbeat and tempo, which encompasses the actions of thinking, believing, talking, and doing that which keeps the organization marching in unison.

- Leadership, is all about COMMUNICATION, COMMUNICATION, COMMUNICATION.

****

**"Do not block the sunshine
of life's today
With the clouds of
life's yesterday."
~ARN~**

****

**It is not enough to
see the possibility,
You must become the
possibility.**

****

Let my actions speak for me
instead of me speaking of my actions,
especially if my actions are not yet realized.
Arthur R. Nicholson (Jan 1994)

Chapter 15

The Vision Becomes Reality

(The rolling O)

At three months and counting to game time, things seemed to be shaping up, and the vision was becoming clearer to all. Most of the mini inspections and oversight-visits, by higher headquarters, did help to focus our energy in the right direction, although at times it felt more painful than helpful. That said, we endured, and were in a better place for it at game time. The assessment that we relied on most was our own internal self-inspection program. It had proven itself predictable and reliable in that it had predicted the previous inspection failure within +/- 3 points. After learning this, I directed the program managers to ensure that we were procedurally correct in our processes, and that accurate documentation was being captured. If we did that, I felt that all else would take care of itself. Of course, that was easier said than done given that Murphy's law seems to come into play when you least expect it. Lesson learned, always expect Murphy's law (anything that can go wrong will).

Overcoming Obstacles

When I was in high school, I memorized the following poem which resembled the struggles that we were going through as an organization. I often reflected on this poem along this journey.

Dancing On The Razor's EDGE

When things go wrong, as they sometimes will,
When the road you're trudging seems all uphill,
When the funds are low and the debts are high,
And you want to smile, but you have to sigh,
When care is pressing you down a bit,
Rest if you must-but don't you quit.

Life is queer with its twists and turns,
As everyone of us sometimes learns,
And many a failure turns about
When he might have won had he stuck it out;
Don't give up, though the pace seems slow
You might succeed with another blow.

Often the goal is nearer than
It seems to a faint and faltering man,
Often the struggler has given up
When he might have captured the victor's cup.
And he learned too late, when the night slipped down,
How close he was to the golden crown.

Success is failure turned inside out
The silver tint of the clouds of doubt
And you never can tell how close you are,
It may be near when it seems afar;
So stick to the fight when you're hardest hit
It's when things seem worst that you mustn't quit
                    Betty Rich (Benedetta Naimo-LaRiccia)

I also read about individuals who had overcome obstacles in their lives and became champions. One such person who surely overcame adversity, and that I most admire, is Mrs. Wilma Rudolph, a 1963 Olympic track star. Wilma Rudolph was born and raised in Clarksville, TN, my hometown; and I had the honor, and pleasure of knowing her, and her family. She became a track star, going to her first Olympic Games in

158

1956 (the year I was born) at the age of 16. That year she won a bronze medal in the 4x4 relay. Mrs. Rudolph qualified again on September 7, 1960, in Rome. She also became the first American woman to win three gold medals in the Olympics. She won the 100-meter dash, the 200-meter dash, and ran the anchor on the 400-meter relay team. I enjoy reading stories about overcomers, and Mrs. Rudolph was just that. She was born prematurely, weighing only 4.5 pounds; the 20th of 22 children. For several years, Wilma endured one illness after another: measles, mumps, scarlet fever, chicken pox and double pneumonia. Then it was discovered that her left leg and foot were becoming weak, and deformed. She was diagnosed with polio, a crippling disease that had no cure. Wilma's mother was told that Wilma would never walk.

Wilma's mother did not accept that answer, and took her to Meharry Hospital, the black medical college of Fisk University in Nashville, TN, twice a week for two years, until she was able to walk with the aid of a metal leg brace. Through a lot of hard work by Wilma and the entire family, finally, by age 12, she could walk normally, without crutches, brace, or corrective shoes. It was then that she decided to become an athlete. Even if I had never known Wilma, this story of her overcoming, against all odds, would resonate with me on the deepest levels. As a child, I saw first hand the children that had to wear those braces to correct their deformities. Of course, when Wilma was making her fame I had no idea of the challenges that she had overcome. However, to know those who endured the same afflictions that she overcame, makes her story all the more real, and deeply motivating for me. I tell that story because when the times in my life get tough (Murphy's Law), I think about how much worse it could really be.

Murphy's Law on Overtime

From January to June of 2008 my leadership skills, and the entire organization's resolve was put to the test, and our existence was truly a "Dance On The Razor's EDGE." Because we were so focused on the IMR statistics and the processes that supported them, other readiness statistics started falling through the cracks. To ensure that we caught any significant movement in all of the statistics, I directed that I be made aware of any statistics that showed a +/- 5 percent movement, and any statistics that dropped below 85 percent was an emergency situation.

Well, it so happened that I was notified that our training statistics were going to dip to 50 percent because most of our personal training statistics were going to expire. In most cases, this was because mass training had been conducted two years prior in preparation for the failed inspection. I called an emergency meeting of the executive committee to look at possible courses of action. We decided that we would have to commit the unit to an extra weekend in February for additional training. To make this happen, we had to request extra funding and prove that it made sense to commit funds to this effort, as there were competing operational missions. This last six months was like running a 440 relay, and on the last lap having to jump hurdles to finish the race. We cleared the first hurdle and our training statistics were back up over 85 percent by the end of February.

Next came system changes in tracking and recording our training database, that we had gotten so comfortable with analyzing and projecting from. Just when we had gotten back to above the 85 percent level, the whole system changed. My hat is off to the men and women who worked night and day to ensure that we stayed in compliance through the inspection period. They devised excel spreadsheets offline to stay abreast of our status until all of the data in the legacy system could be loaded into the new database and verified. This was a daunting task, and they stayed the course. This effort was evidence that LAP was alive and well in the organization. It was also evident that the first line leaders took ownership in their processes, and made it happen.

It did not end there. The system that tracked the IMR statistics for the entire Air Force Reserves crashed around April, 2008, three months before the inspection, throwing everyone into a world of hurt. This was the one statistic that we had worked on all year to get compliant, and now there was practically no way to know where we were three months before going into the inspection. To put it into perspective, we had approximately 1,300 members, with an average of 10 to 15 data points per member to keep track of at any given point (approximately 20,000 data points). Murphy's Law was working overtime at this point in the game. Our saving grace for documentation was that we had a copy of a pie chart of the whole Wing that showed us at 73 percent just prior to the system crashing. By this time, everyone, including me, was at his or her wit's end. Adding to our plight was a newly rolled out HSI Inspection Program that was much more stringent in its scoring criteria, which we had to learn and apply to our own internal inspection evaluation. Everyone asked, "What else could happen before the inspection?"

If you have been keeping track, you know that I usually made a speech during the Saturday morning meeting just before we started the physical examination process. The intent of the meeting was to apprise everyone on the current agenda, and address any issues that would affect our weekend objectives. My goal/roll as the Commander was to welcome everyone back, recognize any newcomers, address any high level issues, and be done in fifteen minutes or less. After all, I had a Commander's Call scheduled each month to address any of my specific concerns. Nevertheless, given all that we had gone through to this point, and the feeling throughout the organization, I felt compelled to make my now famous (at least in the unit) "No Excuses" speech. None of my talks were preplanned, save for the topic, because they just happened based on my sense of the energy in the organization. We had experienced a lot in the last four months, and the energy was low, but we had two months to go before the inspection in June.

That morning, April, 2008, the unit experienced, from me, what they had never quite seen before; an outpouring of passion for achieving our goal that was quite unexpected, even to me. As I started talking I started pacing, because my energy level was so high. I also made eye-to-eye contact with just about everyone in the room that day. What I was doing was almost uncontrollable because of my passion for the people, and the vision to which we had committed so much. I started talking about my life experiences/struggles and not accepting or making any excuses about where I was at that point in my life. I declared that we as an organization must not make any excuses about where we were at this point in our quest to exceed any expectations regarding the inspection. I expressed to them that I knew that they did not take me seriously when I first shared with them that we could achieve an outstanding score, and be a part of something great. Then, I made sure that they knew that having gotten to know each of them over the last sixteen months, shed any doubt in my mind of our collective potential to meet our goal.

There was much more said, and when I finished, two things had occurred. I had gone over my time, and I had very much surprised myself with regard to my performance. In fact, when I finished, I was shaking from the intensity of the speech. There was nothing but silence for a few seconds after I finished. I think everyone was as surprised as I was, and needed to collect themselves. Then came the chants, 459th AMDS, The Committed Few, Practicing LAP, a Part of Something Great! It was like witnessing the beauty of formation flying; priceless. I was told, after the inspection, that particular speech put the nail in the coffin of doubt and hesitancy for everyone. It in turn inspired everyone to a new energy level that galvanized and sustained the organization throughout the inspection.

Fortunately, no other incidents occurred. We regrouped using old school techniques, putting pencil to paper, and tracking all of the statistics the best we could. Everyone including higher headquarters, and our inspectors were in the same boat (or sinking ship) with respect to seeing our last data point in the system. That knowledge put us at ease to know that we only had to maintain where we were until a new system was in place, and that did not happen until after the inspection.

Life Comes At You Fast

Life comes at you fast, and we were experiencing it at warp speed in our preparation for the inspection. It was now May, one month before the inspection, and we started a mad dash for the finish line. There is a time to prepare and a time to be tested, "all things in time" as the saying goes, and we felt that all things were happening at the same time. Fortunately, we had prepared for the pressures that are associated with a race to the finish. We had conditioned ourselves for the long race. The dividends of practicing LAP throughout the year paid off when things seemed insurmountable; and I was proud that our leaders kept level heads and figured out a way to make it happen.

Words can hardly describe the amount of energy and sacrifice that goes into getting ready for an inspection of the type that we were about to face. This inspection would literally determine our fate to exist as an organization. To put it bluntly, everything was on the line. When you are in this place, leadership is everything, and everyone has to be a leader. The committed few became the committed many, and their hard work and enthusiasm became a launching pad for the highest of expectations going into the inspection. Our internal assessment was designed to reflect our scores by element and category from the previous inspection, and to reflect our objective scores, and actual assessment scores. The possible scoring that an organization could achieve on the inspection was unsatisfactory (< 70%), marginal (70-79%), satisfactory (80-87%), excellent (88-92%), or outstanding (93-100%). We were to be evaluated on 42 elements, in six different major areas.

I personally inserted myself into the evaluation process (trust and verify). I mandated that program managers know their respective inspection elements, and that all documentation supported their self-assessed scores. We meticulously reviewed and verified all elements and supporting documentation. By all accounts, our conservative assessment showed a score of 96 percent +/- a 3 percent error rate. A very interesting thing happened next, which is indicative when one has experienced failure in the past. Self-doubt crept in against all evidence that we were actually as good as we had assessed.

This was a critical leadership moment. A leader has to seize the opportunity to calm this self-doubt, which is really nervous energy that is naturally experienced, and, in fact to some extent, is good to have before a contest or battle. I recognized that part of the self-doubt was the hesitancy to believe and accept the fact that our hard work and perseverance for the past 17 months was paying off. In short, some could not believe that we could or would score that high on the actual inspection.

Leaders must recognize the negative energy of self-doubt in their followers/leaders, and transform them into believers of their own fate. It is our charge to help them realize that the vision is real, and ripe for the taking. Of course, this atmosphere in the organization called for one last speech. At one month before the inspection, this speech had to be about sustaining the effort, anchoring the faith that it could be done, and letting them know how proud I was to be associated with such a hard working, dedicated group of individuals. Basically, this was the rallying speech, and I sincerely meant every word of it. In essence, I explained it this way, "We did, therefore we can; and it is possible."

After that particular speech, I went back to my office and wrote then what has become the title of this book. With everything that had happened, the thought came to me that this experience was like dancing on the razor's edge. Everyone was feeling that way. I actually wrote the phrase down on a post-it note on 31 May 2008, five days before the inspection, and stuck it on my in-out box on my desk.

The Inspection

It was now June and in flying terms, we were on short final for touch down. The actual inspection started on Thursday, 5 June, and lasted for three days, with an out-brief scheduled for Sunday, 8 June, 2008. The 5th of June finally arrived and after a short in-brief, the inspectors used the whole of the first day inspecting documentation.

The in-brief to the inspection team was just as significant as my first briefing with the entire unit. Major Connelly and I briefed in a tag team fashion, he briefing the strategic plan and statistics leaving me to brief the overall health of the unit. We knew that we had to show presence, confidence in our programs, and confidence in our personnel. The in-brief was a defining moment of the inspection, as it laid a solid foundation for a very collaborative atmosphere between the inspectors and the unit members. At the end of each day, the inspectors gave a brief account of their findings. The second and third day involved interviews of program managers to verify findings discovered from document reviews and explore additional areas of concern. After each element inspection and interview, our program managers would report to our inspection program manager with the score that they felt was received.

During the first day of document review, not much additional documentation was asked for by the inspectors, which was a good sign, and our feelings were confirmed in the out-brief. We were feeling pretty good about that. On these types of inspections, one thing you do not want to happen is to have a major program failure or a repeat finding, and we were very sensitive to ensure both did not happen. Now for the drama of Murphy's Law; the second day was going along uneventful until a finding showed up that could potentially be a bombshell. When this happened, the team circled the wagons and pulled out all of the stops to ensure that any damage done was minimal. The second day ended with the drama seemingly corralled to avoid a major program finding. The same thing happened on the third day of the inspection. We did everything that we could to present and defend our position with documentation, regulations, and conversations, to the best of our ability. That Saturday night, with the documentation verification and interviews completed, the inspectors huddled to come up with an overall score and write their preliminary executive evaluation.

Licking Our Wounds

The executive committee also huddled to assess where we thought we were, given all that had transpired. When you are passionate about a thing, as we were about our efforts and programs, the thought of getting less of a score than we had conservatively assessed was a heavy feeling and hard to swallow. That Saturday night, needless to say, we were all spent because we knew that we had left it all on the field. Most of us met at the club on base just to unwind, talk, and ponder our fate. After awhile, I thanked everyone for an outstanding effort over the past 18 months. I then told them that whatever score we received, I knew what they had done and the effort they had put forth; and I was very proud and honored to have served with them.

Then I did as I had done almost every month on Sundays after the end of our drill weekends, I stopped by an Air Force base nearby that had a dock area to watch the boats on the Potomac and the airplanes flying in and out of Reagan National Airport. This place was always very calming for me as I collected my thoughts about the events of the weekend. What it felt like that night was akin to being back in that peewee game with me on third and being the winning run to end the game. The difference was that I had to wait a whole night until I knew if we, not I, scored and won the game.

Mission Impossible Accomplished

The next day was Sunday and there was a set procedure of how the score was to be revealed. The team chief of the inspection team was to meet with me at 10 a.m. to go over the evaluation and the score. Then at 1030 a.m. we were to proceed to the Wing Commanders' office to brief her, after which we would proceed directly to the auditorium and brief the entire unit. At no time after I was briefed could I reveal the score to anyone before the score was revealed to the entire organization. I arrived at the office particularly early since I could not sleep the night before. I think I just wanted to get the day started, at least for myself. When I arrived, no one else was there, and there was a peaceful quietness in the halls that morning. It seemed that 10 a.m. took a long time coming, but it did, and the inspection team, with binders in hand, arrived ready to brief.

After the Chief inspector came into my office, closed the door, and sat down, the first thing that she asked me was, what did I think we had scored? I immediately said, "An outstanding." She again asked, what did I think the actual score was? To which I said, "Given our two surprises, I thought we scored a 94." She said, "No, you did not get that," and there was a pause. At that point, even though I knew that I could not show it, my heart dropped to the floor and for the moment I was numb. That feeling was surreal, in that I had been there before, during what I knew to be my last flight as the pilot in command of an Air Force jet. In what seemed like a lifetime, as my past raced across my mind, in the same sentence the Chief Inspector said, "No, you did not get that," She uttered, "You did get a 93, and that is an OUTSTANDING!"

Again, just as in the peewee baseball game, I felt overwhelming exhilaration, and a feeling of accomplishment; all of which I felt a need to somewhat conceal, and show some composure. After hearing the score of outstanding, my first thought after regaining myself was "How great it was going to be for the members to hear it." We had done it! Exactly at 10:30 a.m. we marched over to the Wing Commander's office and broke the news to her. She was also excited, overwhelmed, and proud of the unit because she had endured the failure as much as we had, and in turn given so much support to the turnaround effort.

The Rolling O

Next came the out-brief to the entire unit. We walked from then Col Harris' office to the 459th Aeromedical Evacuation Squadron's auditorium for the final out-brief. I could feel the energy of anticipation from every single person in the room as we walked in. As with protocol, Col Harris led the way into the auditorium, and we took our designated seats. I cannot express how excited and bursting at the seams I was to let it out, but I remained calm showing little outward emotion of how well we had done. Based on our assessment and the daily out-briefs, everyone knew that we had passed, but given the two unexpected findings, we were not sure what the final outcome would be. The Chief Inspector took the stage and wasted no time starting the briefing, explaining each area score. It seemed like a lifetime as she meticulously went through each section giving the methodology of scoring and its impact. When she finished all of the area scores, she paused and asked the members of the 459th AMDS the same question that she had ask me in the office.

Before anyone could say anything (as if they would), the video screen showed something rolling over and over getting larger as it rolled. When it stopped rolling, **OUTSTANDING** showed up on the screen in very large letters, and the entire room erupted. Everyone was jumping up and down, crying, laughing, and overcome with joy, just as in the peewee game. Even as I write this account some four months from its occurrence, I am overwhelmed by the emotions that are stirred up in me. It was so special seeing the elation, excitement, and joy on the faces of our members. I was so happy for all of them. Another peewee game complete, a winning run scored, and it felted soooooooooooooo good! This definitely was the height of my leadership experience, thus far.

Chapter 15 Leadership Takeaways

- Always expect Murphy's law.

- When things go wrong, as they sometimes will,
  When the road you're trudging seems all uphill,
  When the funds are low and the debts are high,
  And you want to smile, but you have to sigh,
  When care is pressing you down a bit,
  Rest if you must-but don't you quit!

- A leader has to seize the opportunity to calm self-doubt, which is really nervous energy that is naturally experienced.

"Dreams are but thoughts yet to be molded into reality. We all dream, but only a few take the initiative to mold those dreams into reality. Only a few leave their secure niche and risk failure in the realization of a dream. Those are the few that succeed. The challenge is for each to take charge of your dreams, and acknowledge that YOU are the single most influential factor in molding your dreams into reality."

Arthur R. Nicholson

Chapter 16

Next!

(Adjusting the vision)

We did it! We worked hard, and the vision became reality. We became a part of something great by coming back from failure, and certain non-existence, to outstanding. I am told that this feat is rare in its occurrence, and the significance of it will only be realized with time. What I do know now, as I realized earlier in life, the experience was a very rewarding yet humbling experience.

The Celebration

This was a time to celebrate the moment, reflect on the past, and refocus on the future. In that moment, we were judged outstanding, and deservedly we did celebrate, for all it was worth. We not only celebrated the victory, we celebrated the individual and organizational growth that took place over the past 18 months. Individuals did find the leader within, and stood up to the challenge when it really counted. In reflecting on the past, I was especially grateful for this accomplishment for those members of the organization that had endured the failure of the past inspection, and stayed the course to experience being a part of something great. To look into their eyes and see the confidence that success breeds, was a far different look than the despair that I saw when I arrived at the unit. I could feel the self-respect that exuded from their walk, and their words of congratulations and thanks to each other. Through the practicing of LAP, discipline, and old fashion hard work, we got that big C-5 aircraft rolling. We created enough thrust to get it off the ground, and set our altitude for outstanding. We stayed on course and altitude until it was determined that "mission impossible" was accomplished. I must say that I am most proud of each person of the 459th AMDS for accepting "mission impossible," and figuring out the way to make it possible. Thanks!

The need to refocus is inevitable if you are to continue to go forward. One should always ask the question, what's next? Refocusing puts eyes on target for that next goal. We realized that we were outstanding for a day, and the reality of a continued service of excellence is born out of a continuous thirst for excellence. Good is not great, and outstanding is not forever.

My Prayer

My prayer is that if you have gotten to this point in the book, you have read, felt, and embraced something that has truly inspired you and changed your vision. My journey to command has been phenomenal in that it has given me the opportunity to engage with some magnificent individuals that have been significant in shaping my life. If you are already in a leadership position, I hope that your fire to lead burns brighter and hotter than before. If you aspire to lead, know that being a servant leader is not the only way to lead, but it is the only way to lead, from a win/win perspective and leave a lasting impression on yourself and those you lead.

****

Strive to be a part of something great!
Find the leader within
Practice LAP
Transform from me to we
Become one of the committed few

****

Chapter 16 Leadership Takeaways

- There is a time to celebrate the moment, reflect on the past, and refocus on the future.

- The need to refocus is inevitable if you are to continue to go forward.

- Good is not great, and outstanding is not forever.

- If you aspire to lead, know that being a servant leader is the only way to lead, (with a win/win perspective), leaving a lasting impression on yourself and those you lead.

Index

459th AMDS, 8,21, 22, 40, 59, 73, 74, 78, 89, 94, 109, 111, 122, 123, 136, 137, 163, 169, 172

459th Air Refueling Wing at Andrews AFB, MD, 21, 23,

4th Air Force, 22, 25, 56, 57

80/20 rule, 92

932nd Aeromedical Staging Squadron (ASTS) 54, 114

A
Accountability, 4, 11, 12, 15, 17, 18, 20, 36, 47, 103, 106, 108, 112, 121, 122, 123, 124, 125, 126, 127, 132, 136, 137

Administrator, 21, 54, 75

Aerospace Medicine Squadron, 14, 21, 24, 71

Air Force Reserves, 56, 136, 161

B
Brigadier General Harris, 7, 23, 24, 26, 40

Bulkhalter, Regina, 8, 25

C
Chief Flight Surgeon, 138

Chin-Ning Chu, 67

Clarksville, TN, 158, 179

Climate survey, 42

Coach Best, 97, 98, 99, 100

Cohen, George, 7, 33

Cohen, William A., 19

Command, 10, 13, 21, 22, 23, 24, 25, 26, 29

Commander, 10, 13, 18, 21, 23, 24, 26, 27, 40, 41, 47, 54, 55, 63, 81, 90, 106, 109, 112, 113, 115, 137, 148, 161, 179

Commitment, 8, 10, 12, 34, 35, 39, 43, 91, 94, 95, 105, 121, 126, 131, 138, 148, 180

Committed Few, 14, 34, 36, 38, 91, 92, 93, 94, 95, 111, 163, 164, 167

Communication, 40, 43, 46, 50,

About the Author

Born in Clarksville, TN, Nick has read and written about motivation, inspiration, and leadership since the age of thirteen. While deployed in Kirkuk, Iraq, he wrote articles on the pressing need of leadership in and out of the war zone.

Nick has maintained dual careers as a Civil Servant with the Federal Government, and as a Reservist in the Air Force. Presently, Colonel "Nick" is the Deputy Director, Executive Services, in the Directorate of the Deputy Chief of Staff, Strategic Plans and Programs, Pentagon, Washington, D.C.

His previous assignment was Commander, 459th AMDS Andrews Air Force Base, MD. He was responsible for the organization, training, equipping and worldwide duty readiness of over 80 squadron members supporting a Wing of 1,300 personnel in 20 units. This assignment became the inspiration for the book Dancing On The Razor's Edge.

Nick has over 34 years of combined enlisted and officer service. He has served in both Kuwait, Saudi Arabia (Operation Desert Storm), and Kirkuk, Iraq (Operation Iraqi Freedom).

As a civil Servant, he has accumulated 26 years of service, and is currently a Senior Contracting Officer, level III certified, with the Federal Government.

Nick is also currently the President and CEO of SIE Global Enterprises LLC, a contract-consulting firm, and SIE Global Publishing LLC, companies grounded in Service, Integrity, and Excellence.

Disclaimer: The information and opinions contained in this book are solely from the author and do not represent the points of view, comments, or support from of any private and or public organization in which the author has served in the past, present, or future.

Notes

[1] William A. Cohen, Ph.D., Major General, USAFR, Retired, "The New Art of the Leader, " Prentice Hall Press, 2000, page xii.
[2] Jeffry F. Smith, Commanding an Air Force Squadron in the Twenty-First Century, August 2003, page 1.
[3] Jeffry F. Smith, Commanding an Air Force Squadron in the Twenty-First Century, August 2003, page vii.
[4] Perry M. Smith, Ph.D, Major General USAF, Retired, "Rules & Tools for Leaders, A Down-to-Earth Guide to Effective Managing," The Berkley Publishing Group, 1998
[5] Presence, http://dictionary.reference.com/browse/presence, September 2008
[6] Commitment, http://www.prismltd.com/commit.htm, August 2008
[7] Trust, http://www.spirithome.com/definif.html, September 2008
[8] Robert K. Greenleaf, Servant Leadership, A Journery into the nature of legitimate of Power and Greatness, Larry C. Spears, Paulist Press, 2002
[9] Employee Climate Surveys, http://www.tesystemsinc.com/ecs.htm October 2008
[10] Brad L. Rawlins, Trust and PR Practice, www.instituteforpr.org/essential_knowledge/detail/trust_and_pr_practice January 2009
[11] Brad L. Rawlins, Trust and PR Practice, www.instituteforpr.org/essential_knowledge/detail/trust_and_pr_practice January 2009
[12] Robert Galford and Anne Seibold, The Trusted Leader, The Free Press, 2002
[13] Robert Galford and Anne Seibold, The Trusted Leader, The Free Press, 2002
[14] Stephen M. R. Covey, Rebecca R. Merrill, The Speed of Trust, Free Press, 2006
[15] Shockley-Zalabak, Pamela, Ellis Kathleen, Winogard, Gaynelle, Organizational trust: What it means, why it matters, http://findarticles.com/p/articles/mi_qa5427/is_200001/ai_n21464956/, January 2009
[16] Shockley-Zalabak, Pamela, Ellis Kathleen, Winogard, Gaynelle, Organizational trust: What it means, why it matters, http://findarticles.com/p/articles/mi_qa5427/is_200001/ai_n21464956/, January 2009

[17] David Viles and Kristian Park, Trust but Verify, http://www.iprisk.co.uk/iprisk2009/documents/Article14.pdf, October 2008

[18] Fields, Ken ""But" vs "And", 3 Feb. 2007.. http://ezinearticles.com/?But-vs-And&id=441222, April 2009

[19] Verify, http://dictionary.reference.com/browse/verify, September 2008

[20] Sharon M. Latour, Vicki J. Rast, Dynamic followership: the prerequisite for effective leadership, http://findarticles.com/p/articles/mi_m0NXL/is_4_18/ai_n9485449/, October 2008

[21] Dr. John Pitron, Followership is LeadershipThe Leadership-Exemplary Followership Exchange Model, http://knol.google.com/k/dr-john-pitron/followership-is-leadership/12nb17zejmb1w/2# October 2008

[22] Five Reasons to Follow, http://changingminds.org/disciplines/leadership/followership/follower_five_reasons.htm, Mar 2009

[23] Sharon M. Latour, Vicki J. Rast, Dynamic followership: the prerequisite for effective leadership, http://findarticles.com/p/articles/mi_m0NXL/is_4_18/ai_n9485449/, October 2008

[24] Dr. John Pitron, Followership is Leadership The Leadership-Exemplary Followership Exchange Model, http://knol.google.com/k/dr-john-pitron/followership-is-leadership/12nb17zejmb1w/2#, October 2008

[25] Sharon M. Latour, Vicki J. Rast, Dynamic followership: the prerequisite for effective leadership, http://findarticles.com/p/articles/mi_m0NXL/is_4_18/ai_n9485449/, October 2008

[26] Sharon M. Latour, Vicki J. Rast, Dynamic followership: the prerequisite for effective leadership, http://findarticles.com/p/articles/mi_m0NXL/is_4_18/ai_n9485449/, October 2008

[27] Sharon M. Latour, Vicki J. Rast, Dynamic followership: the prerequisite for effective leadership, http://findarticles.com/p/articles/mi_m0NXL/is_4_18/ai_n9485449/, October 2008

[28] Sharon M. Latour, Vicki J. Rast, Dynamic followership: the prerequisite for effective leadership, http://findarticles.com/p/articles/mi_m0NXL/is_4_18/ai_n9485449/, October 2008

[29] Sharon M. Latour, Vicki J. Rast, Dynamic followership: the prerequisite for effective leadership,

http://findarticles.com/p/articles/mi_m0NXL/is_4_18/ai_n9485449/, October 2008

[30] Sharon M. Latour, Vicki J. Rast, Dynamic followership: the prerequisite for effective leadership, http://findarticles.com/p/articles/mi_m0NXL/is_4_18/ai_n9485449/, October 2008

[31] Kari L. Kovar, Leaders and Their Followers, The Value of Exemplary Followers, http://www.roosevelt.edu/hr/td/documents/leadersandfollowers.ppt# , Feb 2009

[32] Chin-Ning Chu, Thick Fact Black Heart, The Path to Thriving, Winning & Succeeding, AMC Publishing, 1992

[33] The Lewis Group, Evidence Based Decision Making, http://www2.gsu.edu/~wwwprl/SRC/Evidence%20Based%20Decision%20Making.doc, March 2009

[34] The Lewis Group, Evidence Based Decision Making, http://www2.gsu.edu/~wwwprl/SRC/Evidence%20Based%20Decision%20Making.doc, March 2009

[35] Results-based Management, Treasury Board of Canada Secretariat, http://www.tbs-sct.gc.ca/rma/rbm-gar_e.asp, March 2009

[36] Results-based Management, Treasury Board of Canada Secretariat, http://www.tbs-sct.gc.ca/rma/rbm-gar_e.asp, March 2009

[37] Eric Lewan,Sir Basil H. Liddel-Hart (Strategy, 1954) , http://www.geocities.com/pentagon/bunker/9969/milquote3.html, January 2009

[38] Howard Thurman, http://www.worldofquotes.com/topic/Committment/1/index.html November 2008

[39] Tom Flores, http://www.worldofquotes.com/topic/Committment/1/index.html November 200

[40] Vince Lombardi, http://www.worldofquotes.com/topic/Committment/1/index.html November 2008

[41] F. John Reh, Pareto's Principle - The 80-20 Rule, http://management.about.com/cs/generalmanagement/a/Pareto081202.htm, November 2008

[42] F. John Reh, Pareto's Principle - The 80-20 Rule, http://management.about.com/cs/generalmanagement/a/Pareto081202.htm, November 2008

[43] Richard Koch, The 80-20 Principal, http://www.docstoc.com/docs/2727353/80-20-Principal---Richard-Koch, November 2008

[44] Long Tail vs 80/20, Digital River Developer Resource, http://www.developer-resource.com/long-tail-vs-80-20.htm, January 2009

[45] Michael Fullan, Leading in a Culture of Change, http://www.csus.edu/indiv/j/jelinekd/EDTE%20227/FullanLeadingInACultureOfChange.pdf, March 2009

[46] Meredith Lee, Until One is Committed, http://www.goethesociety.org/pages/quotescom.html, March 2009

[47] Inspired Leadership, "Insights into People who Inspire Exceptional Performance", http://www.berr.gov.uk/files/file10989.pdf, February 2009

[48] Inspired Leadership, "Insights into People who Inspire Exceptional Performance", http://www.berr.gov.uk/files/file10989.pdf, February 2009

[49] Core Values, http://www.nps.gov/training/uc/npscv.htm, February 2009

[50] United States Air Force Core Values, http://www.usafa.af.mil/core-value/cv-mastr.html, February 2009

[51] Curt Cacioppo, Inspiration vs. Influence, http://curtcacioppo.com/archives/913, April 2009

[52] Kevin Barham, Review of Inspirational Leadership, Inspirational leadership: Henry V and the muse of fire, timeless insights from Shakespeare's greatest leader, Richard Oliver, http://docs.google.com/gview?a=v&q=cache:73a9l4SLTrMJ:www.ncsl.org.uk/review-of-inspirational-leadership.pdf+Inspired+leadership+is+change+leadership.&hl=en&gl=us, January 2009

[53] Kevin Barham, Review of Inspirational Leadership, Inspirational leadership: Henry V and the muse of fire, timeless insights from Shakespeare's greatest leader, Richard Oliver, http://docs.google.com/gview?a=v&q=cache:73a9l4SLTrMJ:www.ncsl.org.uk/review-of-inspirational-leadership.pdf+Inspired+leadership+is+change+leadership.&hl=en&gl=us, January 2009

[54] Ruth Haley Barton, The Loneliness of Leadership, http://www.thetransformingcenter.org/pdf/loneliness08.pdf, January 2009

[55] Ammon Campbell, Loney at the Top, http://leadersavvy.blogspot.com/2007/09/lonely-at-top.html, December 2008

[56] W.H. "Butch" Oxendine, Jr. "Are You a Passionate Leader", http://www.lycoming.edu/orgs/senate/Files/ASGAppts/Passionate%20Leaders.ppt#1, December 2008

[57] Norman Vincent Peale, http://www.theotherpages.org/quote-03c.html, September 2008

[58] Randy Komisar, The Monk and the Riddle, Juniper Networks, Leading with Passion, http://anitaborg.org/files/kimperdikou_abi_december_2007.pdf, January 2009

[59] W.H. "Butch" Oxendine, Jr. "Are You a Passionate Leader", http://www.lycoming.edu/orgs/senate/Files/ASGAppts/Passionate%20Leaders.ppt#1, December 2008

[60] Accountability, http://www.answers.com/topic/accountability, November 2008

[61] Deputy Under Secretary of the Army Knowledge Center, About Situational Awareness, http://www.army.mil/armybtkc/focus/sa/about.htm, Jan 2009

[62] Deputy Under Secretary of the Army Knowledge Center, About Situational Awareness, http://www.army.mil/armybtkc/focus/sa/about.htm, Jan 2009

[63] Professionalism, http://www.tsl.state.tx.us/ld/tutorials/professionalism/home.html, October 2008

[64] Stuart Kinsinger, DC, The Set and Setting: Professionalism Defined, Journal of Chiropractic Humanities 2005, http://www.journalchirohumanities.com/Vol%2012/JChioprHumanit2005v12-33-37.pdf, January 2009

[65] Professional Characteristics Demonstrated by the Student Dispositions, http://www.wou.edu/education/teacher_ed/ug-professionalcharacteristics.pdf, September 2008

[66] The Story of Job, http://www.shvoong.com/books/417587-story-job/, January 2009

[67] C-5 Galaxy, http://www.af.mil/factsheets/factsheet.asp?id=84, February 2009